W9-CNL-379

Technology, Education—Connections
The TEC Series

Series Editor: Marcia C. Linn
Advisory Board: Robert Bjork, Chris Dede,
Carol Lee, Jim Minstrell, Jonathan Osborne, Mitch Resnick

The New Science Education Leadership

An IT-Based Learning Ecology Model

EDITED BY

Jane F. Schielack
Stephanie L. Knight

Foreword by Richard Duschl

Teachers College, Columbia University
New York and London

This material is based upon work supported by the National Science Foundation under Grant No. 0083336. Any opinions, findings, and conclusions or recommendations expressed in this material are those of the author(s) and do not necessarily reflect the views of the National Science Foundation.

Published by Teachers College Press, 1234 Amsterdam Avenue, New York, NY 10027

Library of Congress Cataloging-in-Publication Data

The new science education leadership : an information technology-based learning ecology model / edited by Jane F. Schielack, Stephanie L. Knight ; foreword by Richard Duschl.
    p. cm. — (Technology, education-connections, the TEC series)
    Includes bibliographical references and index.
    ISBN 978-0-8077-5343-9 (pbk. : alk. paper)
    1. Science—Study and teaching. 2. Education—Information technology. 3. Leadership. I. Schielack, Jane F. II. Knight, Stephanie L.
    QA11.2.S866 2012
    507.1—dc23   2012005195

ISBN 978-0-8077-5343-9 (paperback)

Printed on acid-free paper
Manufactured in the United States of America

19 18 17 16 15 14 13 12   8 7 6 5 4 3 2 1

In memory of Richard E. Ewing (1946–2007), a visionary scientist, teacher, and learner who made this project possible

Contents

**PART IV.
CONCLUSION: LESSONS LEARNED**   **121**

Foreword

As I write this preface, I am consumed by the challenges facing K–12 Science, Technology, Engineering, and Mathematics (STEM) education in the decade ahead. In July 2011 the National Research Council (NRC) released *A Framework for K–12 Science Education: Practices, Crosscutting Concepts, and Core Ideas*. The *Framework* was handed off to Achieve, Inc. to produce the Next Generation Science Standards (NGSS). The NGSS will accompany the Common Core Standards in English and Mathematics in bringing reforms and a new vision for learning and teaching. In K–12 science education, the reforms and vision involve an alignment of curriculum, instruction, and assessment that will bring about a coherent sequence and progression of science learning both within grades and across grade-bands (e.g., K–2, 3–5, 6–8, 9–12).

The writing and development of the NGSS is well under way. The architecture of learning performances coordinated around science and engineering practices, crosscutting concepts, and core ideas is in place. While the development and roll-out of the NGSS to states and school districts is certainly a complex task, the participants from NRC, Achieve, and the other collaborating organizations (Council of State Science Supervisors, National Science Teachers Association, the American Association for the Advancement of Science) fully recognize that this challenge pales in comparison to the ensuing professional development challenges, challenges that will require effective, sustainable partnerships among scientists, educational researchers and specialists, and school/classroom practitioners.

You hold in your hands a model for how to turn complex partnerships among scientists, educational researchers, and practitioners into effective learning ecologies. This volume is about the emergence of the Information Technology in Science Center's Integrated Professional Development Model (IPDM). The Center's goal was to explore the connections between *doing science* using information technology and *teaching and learning science* using information technology. The driving research question was "How can we adapt the scientists' use of information technology with respect to modeling, visualization, and analysis of complex data sets in ways that can engage grade 7–16 students in similar authentic scientific inquiry?" Through the successful and unsuccessful enactments of the ITS Center Science Learning Communities (SLC), the IPDM emerged.

The ITS Center's guiding frameworks and answers serve as an exemplar for others planning to begin or already engaged with developing partnerships among participants from competing cultures. School/university partnerships and collaborations are firmly part of our current landscape regarding teacher professional development and pre-service teacher education. With the impending roll-out of the NGSS, such partnerships and collaborations will most likely increase as professional learning communities. This volume provides helpful insights on how to plan and execute long-term professional engagement that is situated in topic-specific teaching and learning.

There is much to be learned here. The Texas A&M University ITS Center participants learned how to establish effective partnerships that morphed into productive learning ecologies. The SLC teams of university faculty, graduate students, and grade 7–16 teachers were at the forefront of thinking and engagement in 21st-century skills and in STEM education. There are important lessons to be learned here, too. An interesting theme found in the volume is that of obtaining creative tension. Creative tension emerges from the complex system and synergistic environment provided by the SLC. By necessity, creative tension requires some disequilibrium and novelty within the group(s). Here is how the editors, Jane Schielack and Stephanie Knight, describe the emergence of this creative tension:

> The scientists and their graduate students provided a direct connection to the use of information technology for modeling, visualization, simulation, and analysis of complex data sets in their research. The education researchers and their graduate students provided a view of how the methods of current science research fit into current instructional and curriculum theory in science education. The classroom teachers provided the laboratory for learning, along with their expertise in modifying tools and representations for use with students in the classroom. Working together in problem-based communities, these three very different populations grew into a complex system that resulted in much more than a collection of distinct experiences.

Through ten chapters organized into four parts, we learn about the frameworks, activities, and outcomes of the ITS Center and of the constituent Science Learning Communities. We also learn that successful teams who created the complex systems leading to creative tension did so by:

- Having the right people participate
- Providing a common place for interactions to take place while developing a common history
- Creating a culture apart from others that existed

So I invite you to read on and to learn more for yourself the pragmatics of building learning ecologies that strengthen science education leadership.

—Richard Duschl, PhD,
Waterbury Chair Professor of Secondary Education
Penn State University

Preface

In 2000, a group of people from a variety of perspectives came together to brainstorm ideas for addressing the need for a new generation of science education leaders. This collection of researchers and graduate students in the physical, life, and earth sciences; researchers and graduate students in science education and educational psychology; and grade 7–16 science teachers created an environment of distributed expertise resulting in a set of interactive experiences known as the Information Technology in Science Center for Teaching and Learning (the ITS Center). The ITS Center, presented conceptually in this book as the ITS Learning Ecology, was a Texas A&M University graduate program funded by the National Science Foundation to produce 21st-century science education leaders who could help bridge the gap between current research in science and instruction in science classrooms. After 7 years of working together, we wrote this book about the development of our IT-based learning ecology in order to share what we learned with the hope of inspiring others by providing concrete suggestions for making such collaboration successful.

Bringing authentic scientific inquiry to the classroom has always been a goal for science educators who hope to engage students in the thrill of investigating interesting questions about our universe. The ITS Center focused on the fact that today's and tomorrow's technology brings new perspectives to this effort. The scientists and their graduate students provided a direct connection to the use of information technology for modeling, visualization, simulation, and analysis of complex data sets in their research. The education researchers and their graduate students provided a view of how the methods of current science research fit into current instructional and curriculum theory in science education. The classroom teachers provided the laboratory for learning, along with their expertise in modifying tools and representations for use with students in the classroom. Working together in problem-based communities, these three very different populations grew into a complex system that resulted in much more than a collection of distinct experiences.

The recognition of our *whole* being so much more than the sum of its *parts* drew our attention to the synergy we had developed and the use of ecology as an analogy for our program. We began to see the ITS Center program as an IT-based learning ecology in which individuals from the different populations interacted within heterogeneous learning communities and from which emerged uniquely qualified science education leaders. We have used this analogy throughout the book as a context within which to share our experiences and observations. Differences in tone and voice related to the diverse roles assumed by participants emerge throughout the chapters. Although chapter authors often use similar events and examples to support conclusions about lessons learned, comparison of the unique perspectives of these shared events provides insights into how synergy was created through this diversity.

We see the book being used by various groups involved in science education leadership development. Researchers in both science and science education can use this book for guidelines that should be considered when building a school–university partnership or in other situations that require connecting their research to the classroom. These guidelines can help researchers in science education form stronger ties to the current scientific research that can promote inquiry in the classroom and provide rich environments for further research in the teaching and learning of science. School district personnel, including principals, supervisors, and teachers who are striving for rich science instruction for their students, can find in this book a vision of what that instruction might look like, along with suggestions for how to make it work.

The book can also be used in a variety of contexts. It could be the seminal reading to stimulate ideas at the beginning of a related funded project. It could be used as a text in a graduate seminar, with science graduate students only, education graduate students only, or, preferably, a mix of these students. A group of classroom teachers might want to use it as a focal point for a study group. Or a professional organization that seeks to promote school–university partnerships in science education could build a workshop around it. More generally, the book could even provide guidelines for collaborations formed around other content, for example, partnerships involving distributed expertise across the educational spectrum that focus on the promotion of the study of foreign languages or the formation of public policy.

The book is divided into four parts. Part I could be viewed as the theory behind the concept of an IT-based learning ecology for science education leadership, providing details on the purpose of the project and the conditions necessary for supporting its creation. Part II focuses on logistics—the components of the program that were created and how they were implemented. Part III addresses the impacts of the learning ecology on the various participants, providing views of common examples across chapters from various perspectives. Part IV summarizes the lessons we learned regarding the nurturing of this type of learning ecology.

As with all ecologies, *organisms* and *habitats* related to the ITS Center have changed over time. But with those changes, the impacts of the experiences are migrating beyond the original people and locations. We hope that this book will continue that migration and contribute to the creation of new learning ecologies that bring together the distributed expertise needed to build rich learning environments.

Acknowledgments

We would first like to thank our champions at the national level who recognized our vision and acted as our advocates as we tried to bring our idea to life. We would also like to thank the college faculty from science and education who were willing to take the professional risk of being involved in an originally ambiguous project and the administrators who supported their involvement. We are grateful to the participants who were so willing to share their feedback with us and to our external evaluators who embedded themselves in the project (coming to Texas every July). Their meaningful comments were the foundation of the development of the program and formed the basis of this book. Finally, we would like to express our gratitude to the reviewers of the original manuscript who provided us with insightful and motivating critiques.

Part I

AN IT-BASED LEARNING ECOLOGY MODEL TO DEVELOP SCIENCE EDUCATION LEADERS: THEORY

The folk wisdom about the forest being more than just a collection of trees is, indeed, a first working principle of ecology (from E. P. Odum & G. W. Barrett, in *Fundamentals of Ecology*, 5th ed., published by Brooks Cole, Pacific Grove, CA, 2005, p. 8).

Part I provides the information needed to set the context for the reader for the remaining chapters; it is basically built around the main issue of the need for an IT-based learning ecology that will support the development of a new generation of science education leaders. Chapter 1 describes the vision of a 21st-century science education leader and the main issues related to creating a learning ecology to support a 21st-century science education leadership program. These issues include identifying the components that lead to the necessary synergy in a learning ecology that involves scientists and educators, engaging members of the learning ecology in authentic tasks that promote growth toward the program goals, and supporting networked communities of distributed expertise that maintain the learning ecology. Chapter 2 discusses the components that lead to the creative tension necessary for establishing and maintaining a healthy learning ecology that can support the development of a new generation of science education leaders.

CHAPTER 1

Building an IT-Based Learning Ecology for Science Education Leadership

Jane F. Schielack

Imagine an adult from the middle of the 20th century being transported through time from 1950 to today without the benefit of gradual adjustment to changes in the world. Where might that person find the most familiar surroundings? It would not be in most homes or businesses, where technology provides individual access to nearly instant information and erases the previous limitations of distance and time (Friedman, 2005). If the time traveler were a scientist, familiarity certainly would not reside in the research laboratories of today, with the sophisticated remote data collection and storage capabilities that support the computer modeling and simulation that are used now to replace time-consuming and expensive physical experiments. Unfortunately, an adult from the 1950s or 1960s would very likely feel most comfortable in a secondary school science classroom, where the topics, activities, equipment, and expectations quite often are much the same today as 50 or 60 years ago.

In thinking about this dilemma, a group of scientists, engineers, and science education researchers posed the following questions:

- How can we bring students' experiences in science up-to-date, in order to better prepare them at least as educated consumers, if not also as producers, of scientific information?
- How can we promote diversity in science education leadership, as well as promote the understanding of and interest in science for *all* students, from the perspective of professional development experiences, curriculum, and instructional design (e.g., Lee & Buxton, 2010)?

- And, in particular, how can we adapt the scientists' use of information technology with respect to modeling, visualization, and analysis of complex data sets in ways that can engage grade 7–16 students in similar authentic scientific inquiry?

In the following chapters, we share our conclusion, based on 6 years of data from our experiences in working together, that these questions must be addressed in a long-term sense through a new design for developing science education leadership—a learning ecology within a complex environment in which there is equally valued participation by individuals from various populations. In this complex environment, scientists, education researchers, and education practitioners interact within synergistic learning communities formed around technology-based inquiry experiences.

THE 21ST-CENTURY SCIENCE EDUCATION LEADER

We asked ourselves: What does a 21st-century science education leader look like? In response, we identified the integration of the following components of science education leadership on which to focus:

1. Understanding of current science content and methodologies, including the use of information technology to create visualizations and models and to analyze complex data sets
2. Ability to translate authentic science research into the classroom
3. Engagement in professional activities that contribute to the field of science education

We also agreed to examine these components as they applied to a range of individuals.

The National Science Foundation (2004) defines science education leaders as

> [A] broad array of professionals who educate and support the K–12 instructional workforce. These professionals include university scientists, mathematicians, and/or engineers who prepare future teachers either in discipline or education courses; local and state supervisors and curriculum coordinators; informal science educators; education researchers; curriculum developers; assessment and evaluation professionals; and school administrators (e.g., principals). (p. 7)

With these various populations in mind, consider the following descriptions of the types of new science education leaders we had in mind as we developed our program.

MT is a general science teacher with several years of experience in a secondary school where more than half of the students qualify for a free or reduced-price lunch. More than half of the students in the general science courses in this school speak English as a second language. MT's students are growing a variety of knock-out mutations of *Arabidopsis* plants and using time-lapse digital photography to generate and test hypotheses about genotype–phenotype relationships. An international plant biology research organization provides the plants, and the students use the Internet to report their results back to this organization to be included in the international database. MT's students come in at lunch and before and after school to keep an eye on their research projects. Pictures of the students with their research projects appeared in the local paper. MT designed and implemented a classroom research project for a master's thesis on the impact on the students' learning and has shared the results at various conferences.

PD is a former high school physics teacher and recent recipient of a doctorate in science education. While writing articles based on dissertation research and applying for science education research positions, PD is teaching introductory physics courses for pre-service elementary teachers and presenting workshops for in-service teachers. PD is incorporating technology in these professional development experiences in which teachers use integrated video and spreadsheet software to record, measure, and analyze data from a physical phenomenon like a bouncing ball or a swinging pendulum. The technology allows all students to collect and analyze data from the same phenomenon to compare results. They can use the technology to repeat it as many times as necessary, avoiding the inconsistencies encountered when using a real bouncing ball without the technology. PD is working with a mathematics education doctoral student and a biology professor to apply this same technology to create mathematical models of the growth of plants and to design related mathematical modeling activities for high school students.

GA is a doctoral student in geology and oceanography. As a science graduate student, GA, along with other graduate student colleagues, is responsible for teaching several lab sections that accompany the freshman earth science courses. GA is interested in learning more about how students learn science and has involved the other teaching assistants in scientific research in education, trying out different instructional approaches and collecting data to compare their effectiveness (e.g., using physical models vs. modeling with technology). GA has presented and published the results of the classroom research in geology education venues and is being actively recruited by science departments that are interested in undergraduate curriculum development.

Professor C is a science professor who teaches at a major research university and is a contributing member on several externally funded, multi-institutional interdisciplinary research projects. This professor is very interested in sharing the excitement and societal impacts of the work in these research projects but must do it in a way that fits into a rigorous research schedule. Therefore, Professor C spends about 2 weeks out of every academic year and 3 weeks in the summers interacting with an interdisciplinary science education research group that includes other scientists, science graduate students, science education graduate students, science education research faculty, and grade 7–16 science teachers. Influenced by this interaction, Professor C has redesigned the curriculum for an undergraduate science course (as a result of doing a personal concept-mapping exercise), set up a web interface where secondary science students can interact with current research data from the interdisciplinary projects, and developed a new awareness of and respect for the process of designing effective instruction based on learning theory and feedback from valid assessment. Professor C says that planning new instructional techniques, gathering data to see how well they work, and using the data to revise the instructional planning is very similar to the process used in the science laboratory to develop, test, and revise hypotheses.

Professor L is a professor of science education who is engaged in research and teaching at a major research university and is very active in several national professional communities. Professor L partners with Professor C in planning the summer interdisciplinary experience. As a result of their work together, Professor L and Professor C are serving on each other's graduate students' committees and have written and submitted several collaborative grant proposals. Professor L's interactions with Professor C in a rich science research context has provided opportunities to form and explore new and more complex theories regarding the learning and teaching of science, including both content and processes.

Each of these individuals is representative of a potential population—education practitioner, education or science graduate student, and education or science professor—from which can emerge science education leaders for the future. The challenge is to provide an environment that will support the emergence of such individuals from a complex system of interactive communities. The concept of a learning ecology resulting from interactions among engaged participants within a rich environment provides a useful analogy for the design of a program to produce 21st-century science education leaders.

THE ITS LEARNING ECOLOGY FRAMEWORK

The purpose of this book is to present what we learned about the general aspects of an IT-based learning ecology that we hope might be applicable to a variety of science education leadership development situations. However, certain details related to our specific project, the ITS Center at Texas A&M University, provide a framework within which to discuss the broader concept of the ITS Learning Ecology. In 2001, the National Science Foundation funded the ITS Center as one of the first two Centers for Teaching and Learning (CTLs) to increase numbers of doctoral graduates in mathematics and science education. Over the next 6 years, in three 2-year cohorts, nearly 200 participants engaged in some part of the ITS Center experience. Interested individuals—including science graduate students, education graduate students, and grade 7–16 science classroom teachers (identified as practitioners)—submitted an application to become a member of an ITS cohort. An individual then became a participant in the ITS Center project based on a faculty committee's review of the individual's application in terms of preparedness for science education leadership development, including years of teaching, prior professional development, and facility with technology. Practitioners from school districts with high percentages of underserved populations were especially encouraged to apply. The diversity of the participants themselves consisted of a fairly even distribution of male and female, with 9% Black, non-Hispanic; 10% Hispanic; 77% White, non-Hispanic; and 4% Other.

The ITS Center activities were planned and implemented by a management team made up of 10 to 16 members at various times: the project's director, other principal investigators, other faculty from science and education who were partially supported by the project and who had an interest in directing its activities, a funded post-doc, the internal and external evaluators, and one graduate student to represent the funded graduate assistants. Faculty, graduate students, and practitioners engaged in ITS Center activities in the context of small heterogeneous groups called Science Learning Communities (SLCs). These SLCs formed around current research being conducted by the scientists in the program that could connect to science curricula for grades 7–16. Each SLC also used an emerging information technology (IT) to support modeling, visualization, or interaction with complex data sets.

As a member of one of these SLCs, each participant experienced the ITS Center's Integrated Professional Development Model (IPDM), to explore the connections between *doing science* using information technology and the *teaching and learning of science*. The IPDM consisted of two 3-week on-campus professional development institutes, one in each of two consecutive summers, to support the development and investigation of IT-based authentic science lessons. During the first summer institute, each participant designed a Student Inquiry Framework (SIF) to be implemented in a classroom setting during the following academic year as a pilot project for incorporating information technology into some aspect of teaching, learning, and doing science. During the second summer institute, each participant designed a Practitioner Research Plan (PRP) to implement along with the SIF the following academic year in order to gauge the impact of the SIF on some aspect of students' learning.

As the ITS Center matured, some participants extended their participation in the ITS Center after their cohort ended by becoming a Campus Resource Person (CRP) and contributing to the planning and implementation of the activities for following cohorts. In general, these CRPs represent the product of the ITS Center—the new science education leaders who have developed within an environment consisting of activities and a shared research agenda that are based on the integration of science, technology, and education—an IT-based learning ecology.

THE ELEMENTS OF AN IT-BASED LEARNING ECOLOGY

Our analysis of the development of science education leadership from the perspective of the organization of individuals (or organisms) from various populations forming higher-level communities within a rich environment connects directly to the basic definition of ecology, "the study of the environmental house [that] includes all the organisms in it and all the functional processes that make the house habitable, (Odum & Barrett, 2005, p. 2). The creative tension produced by the necessity to form varying configurations of expertise matched to tasks and goals, to develop cross-cultural understanding, and to design structures to integrate research and education serves as a catalyst for leadership development. What are the elements of an IT-based learning ecology for developing 21st-century science education leaders that can create and address this desired creative tension?

Populations Involved in Creating New Leaders in Science Education

The critical populations in this learning ecology are researchers and graduate students in both science and education and experienced practitioners in grade 7–16 classrooms, working together within a synergistic environment from which science education specialists emerge as new leaders in science education (see Figure 1.1).

Each of these populations represents a set of collective properties that exist in the learning environment. The members in each of these groups bring necessary expertise to the program. The science researcher, while acting as mentor to the science graduate student participants, provides content knowledge as well as expertise in leading-edge research involving uses of information technology for modeling, visualization, and analysis of complex data sets. The science graduate student models science research processes and identifies potential uses of information technology in those processes. The science education researcher, while acting as mentor to the science education graduate students, contributes research-based curriculum knowledge and expertise in research design to help

Figure 1.1. Emerging New Leaders in Science Education

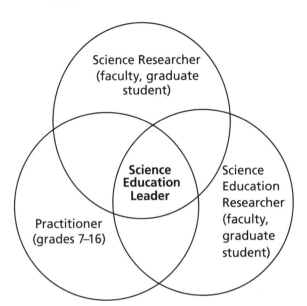

determine ways to effect change in the education process. The science education graduate student identifies and investigates key research questions related to the effects on student achievement of the use of information technology in learning and teaching science. And, as the motivation for the creation of the interdisciplinary environment, the practitioner brings reality from the actual science classroom, including racial, ethnic, and gender diversity, and acts as a catalyst for change by sharing professional growth experiences with his or her peers.

However, these collective properties "do not involve new or unique characteristics resulting from the functioning of the whole unit" (Odum & Barrett, 2005, p. 8). Common experiences in a rich environment are needed to move individuals from the collective properties of the populations to the emergent properties of new science education leadership.

Synergistic Inquiry Experiences for Creating New Leaders in Science Education

A productive learning ecology is built around a clear set of learning goals for the participants. In a program for developing new science education leaders, we want science education graduate students to leave with a better understanding of current science research; more experience with the use of information technology for creating and analyzing models, visualizations, and complex data sets in order to do that research; and insight into possible research questions about teaching and learning science. We want science graduate students to leave with a better understanding of how to communicate their research to the general public and students with various demographics and cultural backgrounds, either in their current teaching assistantship positions or in future faculty positions, and how to gather evidence about the effectiveness of their teaching. We want grade 7–16 practitioners to experience both science and science education research that is relevant to their everyday decision making in the classroom. The model in Figure 1.2 is a compilation of these goals, with the overall learning goal of the ITS program being to move participants toward innovation in both science and education (up and to the right in the figure) from whatever stage they begin at: awareness, experience, or application. The ideal science education leader, described by the far upper-right-hand corner, would be able to conduct equally valuable research in both science and science education. The reality is that this ideal leader in science education might not be a practical goal. However, it *is* a practical goal for scientists and their graduate students moving along the vertical axis to gain a little horizontal momentum by experiencing the scholarship of teaching and learning science, just as we want science education researchers and their graduate students to gain vertical momentum by building their understanding of science research as they move along the horizontal axis of their main specialty.

Figure 1.2. Learning Trajectory for New Leaders in Science Education

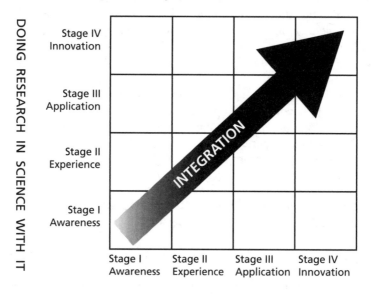

And, in order to move toward achievement of the overall goal for all groups involved, it is critical for them to be able to work in an environment that supports scholarly experiences in both science and education, experiences that often seem physically, as well as conceptually, orthogonal in terms of time needed, behaviors valued, and products expected. Chapter 4 outlines the practical details of designing and implementing such a set of experiences.

Communities for Creating New Leaders in Science Education

According to Odum and Barrett (2005), when discussing the emergent property principle of a complex system, "an important consequence of hierarchical organization is that as components, or subsets, are combined to produce larger functional wholes, new properties emerge that were not present at the level below" (p. 7). The design of the environment for creating new science education leaders must encourage the development of synergy among the populations involved, so that participation in the ITS or a similar program provides benefits that cannot be achieved merely through an accumulation of separate experiences outside of the program. Heterogeneous working groups (the SLCs) provide a rich environment in which interdisciplinary interactions can take place around meaningful problems related to current research in science. The members of a typical SLC consist of one or more faculty who do research in science, one or more faculty who do research in education, graduate students in both science and education, and practitioners from grade 7–16 science classrooms.

Within an SLC, participants address an authentic problem from the participating scientists' current research. It might involve modeling basic properties relevant to nanotechnology or making and testing conjectures related to biodiversity within an ecosystem. Table 1.1 summarizes the scientific emphases of our SLCs, the information technology tools they used, and the configuration of the populations involved as a background for discussions presented in following chapters.

As an SLC engages in different components of their problem, each individual brings to the environment special expertise to share with the others. The integrated experience allows each individual to take away a new understanding not only of the expertise of the other individuals, but also of their own. In other words, the synergistic environment causes each individual to change in ways that increase individual *strength* and allow him or her to better interact with others in related environments.

The Role of Information Technology

As noted in Table 1.1, fairly sophisticated information technology was used in the exploration of science in the SLCs to extend human capabilities for data

Table 1.1. Overview of Science Learning Communities

Learning Community	Science Research Emphasis	Information Technology Used	Populations Involved
Energy and Materials	Equilibrium, conservation, and conversion as related to materials	Modeling software Molecular visualization software	6 Practitioners 2 Sci grad students 4 Sci Ed grad students 2 Scientists 1 Sci Ed researcher
Genomics and Imaging (two groups)	Genetic expression effects on phenotype	Video microscopy Time-lapse imaging Webcam video	11 Practitioners 4 Sci grad students 6 Sci Ed grad students 3 Scientists 1 Sci Ed researcher
Landscape Ecology (two groups)	Spatial statistics and web-based virtual ecological inquiry	GIS Excel Live remote video feed 3D imaging software	8 Practitioners 8 Sci grad students 6 Sci Ed grad students 4 Scientists 1 Sci Ed researcher
Macro and Micro Imaging	Dynamics and interrelationships of living things	Live remote video feed Web-based image analysis 3D imaging software	6 Practitioners 3 Sci grad students 6 Sci Ed grad students 2 Scientists 1 Sci Ed researcher
Molecular View of the Environment (two groups)	Atmospheric chemistry and mineral solubility	Geochemical modeling software Excel	17 Practitioners 3 Sci grad students 3 Sci Ed grad students 4 Scientists 1 Sci Ed researcher
Science and Technology at the Nanoscale	Types of forces and their relationship to scale	Digital microscopes Modeling and simulation programs	11 Practitioners 1 Sci grad student 3 Sci Ed grad students 3 Scientists 1 Sci Ed researcher

Table 1.1. Overview of Science Learning Communities (continued)

Learning Community	Science Research Emphasis	Information Technology Used	Populations Involved
Sustainable Coastal Margins	Hydrologic, geologic, ecologic, and social processes	Web-hosted data bases GIS Excel	2 Practitioners 7 Sci grad students 2 Sci Ed grad students 4 Scientists 1 Sci Ed researcher
Visualizing Biodiversity	Biocomplexity at various temporal and spatial scales	Biodiversity database GIS	7 Practitioners 1 Sci grad students 3 Sci Ed grad students 4 Scientists 1 Sci Ed researcher
The Water Environment	Hydrologic processes related to availability of clean water	GIS Excel Web-hosted databases Computer simulations	9 Practitioners 5 Sci grad students 2 Sci Ed grad students 2 Scientists 1 Sci Ed researcher

collection through remote sensing, to visualize complex data sets, and to create and manipulate models and simulations. More accessible variants of these sophisticated technologies were used in the grade 7–16 classrooms to mimic the scientists' work (see Chapter 3). In general, information technology acted as a unifying structure in the environment across the SLCs, promoting discussions beyond the specific science content to the aspects of higher-level thinking involved in inquiry.

THE RESULTS OF AN IT-BASED LEARNING ECOLOGY

What emerges as a result of an IT-based learning ecology for developing 21st-century science education leaders? The highlighted intersection in Figure 1.1 represents the creation of new leaders in science education. These new leaders emerge from a synergistic environment created by purposeful interaction within the context of distributed expertise. They begin as participants with very specialized interests—for example, teaching 10th-grade chemistry or conducting research on Golgi bodies. They bring these special interests to explore an ill-defined but authentic problem, sharing their expertise with and learning from others.

As members of the SLCs are asked to apply their learning within new situations, their science education leadership skills grow. Scientists develop improved ways to communicate about their research and form partnerships across disciplines to further public understanding of science; science graduate students develop research-based philosophies related to the teaching and learning of science that they will be able to take to their future roles as faculty members or public speakers; both scientists and their graduate students gain a better understanding of teaching and learning as areas for research. As a result of working in the SLCs, science education researchers and their graduate students can connect their studies of teaching and learning to current science research venues.

But, beyond the specialized benefits provided to each participating group, the synergistic environment provided by the SLC structure allows emergence of a new type of science education leader—one who acknowledges the similarities between research in science and research in education, who can move easily back and forth between the departmentalized structures that often exist in the academic environment, who is anxious to work with people from a variety of backgrounds to improve the teaching and learning of science, and who is able to share new knowledge that connects research in science and science education.

REFERENCES

Friedman, T. L. (2005). *The world is flat: A brief history of the 21st century.* New York: Farrar, Straus and Giroux.

Lee, O., & Buxton, C. A. (2010). *Diversity and equity in science education: Research, policy, and practice.* New York: Teachers College Press.

National Science Foundation (NSF). (2004). CLT Program Announcement. Retrieved August 18, 2005, from http://www.nsf.gov/publications/pub_summ.jsp?ods_key=nsf04501

Odum, E. P., & Barrett, G. W. (2005). *Fundamentals of ecology* (5th ed.). Pacific Grove, CA: Brooks Cole.

CHAPTER 2

Initiating and Sustaining a Learning Ecology to Produce 21st-Century Science Education Leaders

Carol Stuessy, Jane F. Schielack,
and Stephanie L. Knight

The Information Technology in Science (ITS) Learning Ecology created a workspace for developing new leaders through integrated professional development formed from a synergy between research and teaching in both science and education. The expectation was that university scientists and education researchers, graduate students, and grade 7–16 practitioners would embrace a common goal of *doing research and engaging students* within Science Learning Communities (SLCs), thus adding to the pool of 21st-century science education leaders.

Building an environment with creative tension was a key aspect of this project. Looking back, this creative tension was the driving characteristic of the ITS program as a learning ecology, the organization of individuals (or organisms) from various populations forming higher-level communities within a rich environment. Creative tension arises from disequilibrium and novelty—when tasks or goals require individuals to reconfigure themselves to act in roles that are unfamiliar to them and to adaptively change course when necessary. Creative tension provided the energy needed to solve the complex problems associated with the learning communities as they worked toward their commitments to doing research and engaging students in authentic research. Teaching and learning within the ITS environment led to the identification of conditions necessary to support the creative tension needed to initiate and maintain the learning ecology, including diversity, the ability to reform structures and roles, new understandings of identity and community, and appropriate incentives.

EMBEDDING DIVERSITY

The first condition required to ensure the creative tension needed in a sustainable IT-based learning ecology for creating 21st-century science education leaders is a foundation of multiple aspects of diversity—diversity of individual participants, of communities of participants, of scientific content, of scientific research technologies and methodologies, and of instructional settings. As highlighted in Chapter 10, diversity is necessary to ensure resilience. In the ITS Learning Ecology, as in many professional development projects, establishing diversity within the group of participants was challenging. Recruitment efforts were directed specifically at populations with higher-than-average percentages of Hispanic and Black master teachers, for example, existing professional development cohorts in inner-city districts and small rural schools. All practitioners recruited from these areas had student populations with high levels of cultural and socioeconomic diversity. Participants also varied widely in terms of background experience and years of teaching. Diversity among individuals resulted in rich conversations within the SLCs, extending everyone's benefits from the experience.

Diversity across the SLCs provided aspects of both the novelty and redundancy required in a healthy ecology (see Chapter 10). As an example of novelty, members of the Nanoscale and Biodiversity Learning Communities engaged in very different inquiry experiences involving different science and using different information technology tools from each other (see Table 1.1). However, redundancy emerged within cross-community retreats when diverse members of all the SLCs identified commonalities among their inquiry experiences and built stronger understandings of scientific inquiry and science education from these commonalities.

In general, diversity was embedded and critical in every aspect of the ITS Learning Ecology for initiating and sustaining the creative tensions that led to growth. Management of diversity focused on providing a flexible environment in which the various components could form and re-form in order to contribute most effectively to the learning ecology.

FORMING AND RE-FORMING
STRUCTURES AND ROLES

The second condition to support the creative tension needed to sustain a learning ecology refers to the ability to create and revise different structures and roles supporting different communities of individuals around a given task or goal. To function effectively, a community depends on having the combinations of expertise needed for accomplishing the task or goal. Structures and roles must be able to change to meet the demands of the task or goal addressed.

From the development of the idea for the ITS Learning Ecology, a great complexity arose. In a manner similar to that referred to by Wheatley (1992) describing Prigogine's work on the evolution of dynamic systems, the ITS Learning Ecology had created an environment where disequilibrium and novelty (i.e., creative tension) within each of the SLCs was a necessary condition for the system's growth. Faced with amplifying levels of disturbance, dynamic systems possess innate properties to reconfigure themselves so that they can deal with new information. For this reason, they are frequently called self-organizing or self-renewing systems (Odum & Barrett, 2005). In the case of the ITS Learning Ecology, re-forming occurred through a dynamic, adaptive, and creative process that allowed the notions of workspace and SLC to constantly adjust to fit the needs of its members.

The ITS Learning Ecology was faced with the task of designing new structures like the SLCs to facilitate the translation of doing science research into engaging students in classroom science learning while accomplishing the goal of creating new science education leaders. The new structures became an experiment in progress, undergoing modifications based on feedback through continuous cycles of "design, enactment, analysis, and redesign," similar to the processes described by the Design-Based Research Collective (2003, p. 5). For example, as described in Chapter 4, the structure of the participants' experiences in the ITS Learning Ecology progressed with each implementation into a tighter integration of coursework, science research experiences, employment of graduate assistants as mentors, and task refinement. Depending on their level of involvement, SLCs' opportunities to re-form and re-create ranged from 2 years with one set of members to 4 years with two sets of members. This innovative design of integrated and flexible structures enabled us to create working models centered on SLCs and shared practice.

In addition to occurring as a result of diversity, creative tension also arises when tasks or goals require individuals to act in roles that are unfamiliar to them and to adaptively change course when necessary. The adaptations required for individuals to be active participants in this process were different for each population. The teaching task for scientists, for example, required them to design scientific research experiences for practitioners in ways that would enable the practitioners to translate these experiences for their own students and engage students in similar scientific inquiry. Many of the latest technologies available for use in the scientific laboratory had no counterparts for use in the classroom. Adaptations in equipment and technology were common (see Chapters 3 and 8), with scientists and practitioners working together to design instructional systems that provided solid inquiry experiences for students (see Edelson, 1998).

From the scientific research experience provided by the scientists and science graduate students in each SLC, each practitioner in the community designed a plan for engaging students in a classroom research experience similar to that experienced in the SLC (see Chapter 5). As a result, graduate students, scientists, and education researchers also participated in the design of classroom problems, illustrating one of the enhancements in roles that occurred to address tasks arising in the SLCs. For example, a graduate student in science and a scientist worked together to develop an inquiry experience for an undergraduate soil geology class that led to published papers and a dissertation by the graduate student (McNeal, Miller, & Herbert, 2008; Sell, Herbert, Stuessy, & Schielack, 2006). In another example, a landscape ecologist designed classroom inquiry experiences for his undergraduates that led to a robust research agenda including a dissertation and data for several research papers (Simmons, Wu, Knight, & Lopez, 2005, 2006, 2008). Collaborative classroom-based research yielded a number of research presentations that included a practitioner, science educator, scientists, and graduate students (e.g., Stuessy, Brooks, et al., 2005; Stuessy, Griffing, et al., 2005; Stuessy, Scallon, & Griffing, 2006; Stuessy, Schielack, et al., 2006). A middle school teacher and a university science educator co-published a paper in a leading science education research journal that integrated the structure of the 2-year professional development experience with the teacher's impressions of that experience on her own professional growth (Stuessy & Metty, 2007) and also yielded the teacher's master's thesis (Metty, 2006).

Each of these examples combined scientific research and student engagement within a classroom-based, information technology–rich, classroom inquiry experience that required formulation and reformulation of structures and roles. Classroom practitioners engaged in scientific research; scientists advised classroom practitioners on innovative practice; university educators prepared classroom practitioners to transform their science learning environments to include innovative IT and inquiry-based experiences for their students and to do research on the effects of the innovation on student learning.

CREATING NEW UNDERSTANDINGS OF IDENTITY AND COMMUNITY

The third condition for establishing the creative tension needed to maintain the health of the learning ecology refers to the flexibility of the SLC structure in allowing its members to negotiate and develop new identities through their participation in the learning community. Wenger (1998) discusses social learning as a process by which newcomers in diverse groups come to grow into their places within the group. Members of the SLCs within the ITS Learning Ecology grew with their participation in learning communities dedicated to *doing research and engaging students*. Individuals from public schools, university research laboratories, and educational research settings *apprenticed* others (see Lave & Wenger, 1991) in their SLCs as they taught one another about their respective cultures.

Both expertise and apprenticeship were distributed among members of the group. Perceiving each individual as having the ability to be both an apprentice and an expert, depending on the various roles taken on within the community at different times, allowed for a free exchange of ideas. The ITS Learning Ecology experience provided time for members within their SLCs to teach one another about their resident communities of practice, share ideas and experiences, reflect on the ideas of others, and revise their thinking about what it means to be a learner in a community of learners committed to learning.

Negotiations among members of the ITS Learning Ecology led to enhanced understandings of the challenges and constraints associated with the culture of each individual's work environment. The task of transferring authentic science into the classroom provided a safe topic for individuals to talk freely about what is and is not possible in terms of an authentic design for classroom use. For example, scientists argued that a science task should allow students to experience a quest for new understandings about a particular phenomenon using technology to spur the discovery. Practitioners, however, expressed their concerns about opening the inquiry to include unanswered questions. While familiar to scientists who work in the world of unanswered questions, this approach may create a sense of panic and fear in practitioners. Science classroom learning environments are often based on unspoken conventions and beliefs: Teachers are supposed to know the answers; laboratory experiences generate results that are either right or wrong; hypotheses can be proved; and the scientific method is a series of linear steps that scientists follow. While scientists work in the world of knowledge generation, practitioners may not understand that the tentativeness of science is something that can and should be taught in the science classroom.

Practitioners talk about the constraints of the classroom in much more concrete terms that are quite real: scheduling difficulties associated with 45-minute time blocks; equipment difficulties, with computers available in the computer lab only when keyboarding sessions are not occurring; administrative difficulties related to the prescribed scope and sequence of curriculum topics that must be covered within a certain time period, leaving little time for authentic scientific inquiry; and high-stakes testing pressures to teach only topics appearing on the test. Furthermore, many practitioners do not perceive their classrooms as laboratories where their own personal inquiries about teaching and learning can occur. Practitioner research may not be identified by them or by their school system as a way to improve science learning and teaching. Traditional notions of laboratory science culture and high school science culture met face-to-face in the SLCs.

Each SLC created an environment for representatives from both cultures to learn from one another and transfer that learning into new ideas about ways to enhance teaching and learning in their own environments. For example, a scientist participant explained that the structure of his laboratory had undergone major revision in terms of the ways that graduate students become enculturated into the world of research. A landscape ecologist now includes an authentic on-line inquiry experience in his sections of beginning landscape ecology, exposing approximately 400 students per semester to the world of scientific inquiry. In a corresponding way, a practitioner participating in the ITS Learning Ecology explained that the structure of her assessments of inquiry learning have significantly changed as a result of considering outcomes associated with inquiry, which look much like the outcomes associated with scientific research: new conceptual understandings about the phenomenon, an understanding of science as a way of knowing about the world, and new abilities to apply scientific information in real-world contexts. Education researchers choose new classroom research settings in which to investigate interactions among practitioners, students, and information technologies as students develop scientific proficiencies that involve much more than content mastery.

PROVIDING INCENTIVES

The final condition for sustaining the environment that allows the disequilibrium and novelty that lead to the creative tension needed in this type of interdisciplinary endeavor refers to the provision of incentive structures that are recognized and valued by the communities' participants. A variety of incentive structures are needed to address the different populations involved.

Practitioners perceive the opportunity to apply for grants that provide resources for their classrooms as an important incentive for working with university professors. For example, the middle school teacher who received a grant from an electronics company to purchase a set of small video cameras was able to more effectively engage her students in genomics research. Practitioners also value the recognition they receive as professionals through presentations and publications and the acknowledgment of their skills and knowledge by other professionals. The practitioners involved in designing and presenting symposia at the American Educational Research Association's international conference extended the professional development experiences for themselves and for others. Partnerships with university faculty and opportunities to take graduate classes satisfied the desire for continued education that many of the practitioners held.

University educators also value the opportunities to seek and acquire, in collaboration with school-based practitioners, grants that might not otherwise be available to them. Faculty members who formed collaborations with other members received federal funding for curriculum innovation, instructional material development, graduate student support, and research on innovative teaching and learning environments. Both science and education faculty achieve national recognition through presentations and publication and are rewarded by their disciplines and academic departments for participation in these activities through promotion and tenure. Specific incentives for education faculty include enhanced teaching due to the closer ties to K–12 settings, research opportunities with public school teachers, and involvement of graduate students in implementation and research studies in schools.

Scientists' incentives are similar and becoming more prevalent due to national attention to the quality of undergraduate science education. Scientists also value the opportunity to apply and receive grants that might not otherwise be available to them. With the emphasis on science education mentioned previously, national recognition for leadership in this area is becoming more attractive to scientists. Scientists participating in collaborative, interdisciplinary projects also view positively the enhancement of their teaching, participation in research with an education focus, and involvement of their graduate students in educational activities. Incentives for graduate students include access to positions with differentiated roles, hands-on involvement in broader-impacts research, and revised conceptions of what it means to be a scientist/science educator.

In general, recognition and availability of these incentives are necessary to attract members and sustain involvement in an IT-based learning ecology to produce new science education leaders. In this environment, with the appropriate incentives, scientists can advise practitioners in solving problems of classroom implementation; university graduate students can observe public school classrooms for new insights on teaching and learning; university scientists, with the help of graduate students, can adapt their teaching to include IT and inquiry in their undergraduate classes; and university researchers can extend their grant work to include new interests that arise directly from the learning ecology experience. Through consensual acknowledgment of the legitimacy of their separate communities of practice, new communities can be formed that include free exchange of ideas and energy among science laboratories, public school classrooms, and graduate student learning environments and from which can emerge a broad spectrum of new science education leaders.

REFERENCES

Design-Based Research Collective. (2003). Design-based research: An emerging paradigm for educational inquiry. *Educational Researcher, 32*(1), 5–8.

Edelson, D. (1998). Realizing authentic science learning through the adaptation of science practice. In G. J. Fraser & K. Tobin (Eds.), *International handbook of science education*, Vol. 2, (pp. 317–331). Dordrecht, Netherlands: Kluwer.

Lave J., & Wenger, E. (1991). *Situated learning: Legitimate peripheral participation.* New York: Cambridge University Press.

McNeal, K. S., Miller, H. R., & Herbert, B. E. (2008). The effect of using inquiry and conceptual model development of complex earth systems through the use of multiple representations and inquiry. *Journal of Geoscience Education, 54*, 396–407.

Metty, J. (2006). *A comparative study of authentic student research versus guided inquiry in affecting middle school students' abilities to know and do genetics.* (Master's thesis, Texas A&M University, College Station, TX.)

Odum, E. P., & Barrett, G. W. (2005). *Fundamentals of Ecology* (5th ed.). Pacific Grove, CA: Brooks Cole.

Sell, K. S., Herbert, B. E., Stuessy, C. L., & Schielack, J. (2006). Supporting student conceptual model development of complex earth systems through the use of multiple representations and inquiry. *Journal of Geoscience Education, 54,* 396–407.

Simmons, M., Wu, X. B., Knight, S., & Lopez, R. (2005, August). *Can GIS improve student interest in and conceptual understanding of ecology?* Poster presentation at the annual meeting of the Ecological Society of America, Montreal, Canada.

Simmons, M., Wu, X. B., Knight, S., & Lopez, R. (2006, August). *GIS as a teaching tool in an undergraduate ecology laboratory: Assessing the use of GIS on students; motivation and conceptual knowledge.* Poster presentation at the annual meeting of the Ecological Society of America, Memphis, TN.

Simmons, M., Wu, X. B., Knight, S., & Lopez, R. (2008). Assessing the influence of field- and GIS-based inquiry on student attitude and conceptual knowledge in an undergraduate ecology laboratory. *Cell Biology Education — Life Sciences Education, 7,* 338–345.

Stuessy, C. L., Brooks, L., Bozeman, D., Force, C., Hilding-Kronforst, S., Metoyer, S., & Warren, C. (2005, November). *How do classroom practitioners integrate authentic science laboratory experiences into their science teaching?* A multiple paper set presented at the annual meeting of the School Science & Mathematics Association, Fort Worth, TX.

Stuessy, C. L., Griffing, L., Harbaugh, A., Bozeman, D., Richardson, R., Scallon, Herbert, B. (2005, April). *Authentic scientific research in secondary school classrooms: Some say it can't be done.* Symposium presented at the annual meeting of the American Educational Research Association, Montreal, Canada.

Stuessy, C. L., & Metty, J. S. (2007). The learning research cycle: Bridging research and practice. *Journal of Science Teacher Education, 18,* 725–750.

Stuessy, C. L., Scallon, J. M., & Griffing, L. (2006, February). *Authentic scientific research learning and guided inquiry: A comparison of what eighth graders do and understand about genetics in two inquiry learning contexts.* Poster presented at a Howard Hughes Medical Institute Science Education Symposium entitled *To Think and Act Like a Scientist: The Roles of Inquiry, Research, and Technology.* Texas Tech University, Lubbock.

Stuessy, C. L. (Organizer), Schielack, J., Bozeman, D., Nickles, G., Milam, J., Peterson, S., & Scallon, J. (2006, April). *Scientific inquiry and information technology: Catalysts for innovative and coherent professional development.* Interactive paper symposium presented at the American Educational Research Association, San Francisco, CA.

Wenger, E. (1998). *Communities of practice: Learning, meaning, and identity.* New York: Cambridge University Press.

Wheatley, M. L. (1992). *Leadership and the new science: Learning about organization from an orderly universe.* San Francisco: Berrett-Koehler.

Part II

SYNERGY IN AN IT-BASED LEARNING ECOLOGY MODEL: LOGISTICS

We never educate directly, but indirectly by means of the environment. Whether we permit chance environments to do the work, or whether we design environments for the purpose makes a great difference (from J. Dewey in *Democracy and Education: An Introduction to the Philosophy of Education,* published by The Macmillan Company, New York, 1916, p. 31).

The next four chapters focus on how synergy was created within the ITS Learning Ecology using technology-based inquiry as a focus, integrated professional development experiences, practitioner research, and a shared research agenda. Chapter 3 provides an explication of the elements identified as critical for connecting current science research to current science teaching. The science and education researchers came to agreement on the following two elements as critical: the engagement of students in authentic inquiry and student use of information technology in the form of modeling, simulation, and interaction with complex data sets in order to facilitate the authentic inquiry. Chapter 4 presents a detailed discussion of the expected learning outcomes for the various participants in the ITS Learning Ecology and a presentation of the critical components of the various activities designed to address these learning outcomes. Chapter 5 describes the impacts on the various groups (classroom practitioners, graduate students, faculty) of the design and implementation of a classroom research project as professional development. Chapter 6 presents the rationale for and describes the complexity of a shared research agenda within a synergistic environment, with shared research differing from the implementation of traditional single investigator research in terms of questions asked, methodologies used, and attributions made.

CHAPTER 3

Creating Synergy Through a Focus on Technology-Based Inquiry

Bruce Herbert, Susan Pedersen,
and Jane F. Schielack

One of the most fascinating events in our lives has been observing the cognitive development of our own children. Consider, for example, this exchange while one of our daughters was in the bathtub when she was 3 years old.

"Hi, Anna. What are you doing?"

"I'm pouring water." Anna proceeded to pour water from a large cup into a small cup and then back into the large cup. She seemed to notice that the large cup held more water than the small cup, but that observation didn't hold her interest.

Then Anna covered one of the cups with a washcloth. She tried to pour water into the covered cup. "Wow!"

"What happened?"

"The water went through!" She then tried the experiment two more times, changing the cups she used.

"Why do you think this happened?"

She thought for a moment. "There must be holes in the cloth," she exclaimed.

As well as being a source of parental pride, this exchange was consistent with research that shows children's thinking can be surprisingly sophisticated. Anna engaged in a range of common scientific practices, including formulating a question, designing and replicating an experiment, and developing an explanation based on evidence. What seemed to make her sophisticated reasoning possible was the fact that she was dealing with a developmentally appropriate phenomenon that she found authentic.

Contrast Anna's experience with the learning environment in many K–12 or university science classrooms, where science is approached as a collection of facts, student engagement is focused on completing worksheets, and assessment focuses on recall of facts. These classrooms reflect an approach to science education that emphasizes *what* we know about science instead of *how* we know and *why we believe what we believe* about science. Instructional activities in these classrooms tend to be built around the demonstration of concepts, an approach that is not likely to engage students in the reasoning skills and the exploration of the epistemological beliefs of authentic scientific practice. However, the current systemic reform of K–12 science education seeks the integrated understanding of science by students (Kali, Linn, & Roseman, 2008) and the improvement of student learning through a student-centered, inquiry-based approach (Duschl, Schweingruber, & Shouse, 2007). Implementation of inquiry-based science instruction requires the engagement of students in authentic practices that mimic the practices of scientists: practices such as asking scientific questions and making predictions, gathering and expressing data and evidence, and constructing and reflecting on scientific explanations (Chinn & Malhotra, 2002; Krajcik et al., 1998; Krajcik, Blumenfeld, Marx, & Soloway, 2000). This reform initiative has been codified in national standards documents including *Science for All Americans* (AAAS, 1990), *Benchmarks for Science Literacy* (AAAS, 1993), *National Science Education Standards* (NRC, 1996), and *Taking Science to School* (NRC, 2007).

In the development of our learning ecology for developing science leaders, we agreed that we wanted to encourage everyone to continue to question like the preschooler who is wondering how the water gets through the cloth that looks like it is solid. We want everyone to be as interested in practicing inquiry as she was in experimenting with different arrangements of materials and liquids to try to answer the questions that we are curious about and that can lead us to a better understanding of the world around us. Therefore, we decided that, for an IT-based learning ecology model of science education leadership to function effectively and efficiently to support improvement in grade 7–16 science education, the members must all have a shared goal of promoting this type of inquiry and of engaging in authentic scientific inquiry themselves, no matter their field or area of interest or expertise.

CREATING INQUIRY-BASED SYNERGY THROUGH SCIENCE LEARNING COMMUNITIES

To facilitate the implementation of this common goal of inquiry, we created the representation in Figure 3.1, illustrating the interconnections among the various components of the desired IT-based learning ecology. As is often the case, the process of designing the image was even more educational than the resulting image itself. In our discussions of the components, we encountered issues that needed to be resolved. For example, how did we want to name the categories of

Figure 3.1. Inquiry-Based Synergy in the ITS Learning Ecology for Science Education Leadership

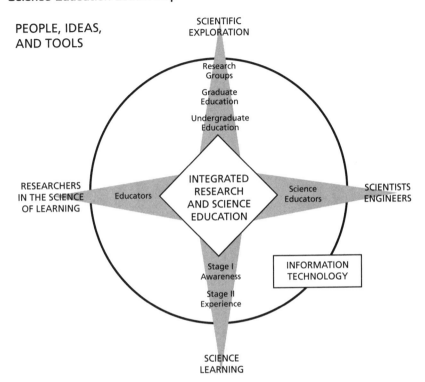

people involved? How could we best describe different levels of scientific inquiry across a spectrum? Each of these seemingly simple vocabulary issues led to some important insights into the creation of synergy within the group, as well as to a more representative image. And, just as the Information Technology in Science (ITS) Learning Ecology evolved across time, the image was revised as the project matured.

As the labels in Figure 3.1 indicate, the representation of the ITS Learning Ecology was designed to (1) capture the spectrum of inquiry involved, from development of theory in science education, through applications in informal and formal settings, to creation of new knowledge in the sciences; (2) highlight the various groups of people involved, including researchers in science and education and educational practitioners; (3) point out the role of information technology in bringing together the various groups of people and targets of inquiry; and (4) create a place through the integration of these components in which to situate the emergence of new science education leaders.

The vehicle by which we sought to bring together these multiple components of the ITS Learning Ecology was the formation of a set of Science Learning Communities (SLCs), small heterogeneous groups (as described in Chapter 1) that each participated in a *synergistic inquiry experience*. (See Chapter 8 for more details on specific SLCs.) We recognized that in order to meet the goals of this project, participants had to bring together diverse bodies of knowledge, including the nature of science, learning theory, assessment practices, information technology (IT), and science content knowledge. Teams of science and engineering faculty were recruited to provide access to the range of areas of expertise practitioners would need in order to be able to transfer the authentic practices of scientists to their classrooms. These teams were therefore interdisciplinary, with faculty and graduate students from different areas of science working together to design inquiry experiences with the help of science education faculty and graduate students. For example, one SLC included a geologist and three chemists; another included a landscape ecologist and a biologist; and a third included a civil engineer, a physical geographer, and a geophysicist.

With relation to inquiry, a scientist's participation in an SLC was two-fold. Foremost, the scientists brought to the group both aspects of their specific area of scientific inquiry (e.g., ways to collect and analyze water-quality data, methods for representing the motion of nanoparticles, observations of samples of deep-ocean cores) and their experience with general inquiry processes that are common across areas of scientific research (e.g., formulating researchable questions, designing ways to make appropriate measures and collect data, analyzing and interpreting results). Second, the scientists worked with the practitioners on the team to design classroom inquiry experiences that would allow the grade 7–16 students to contribute data to authentic research projects. For example, a group that focused on assessing environmental risk factors was able to contribute to the development of a museum exhibit on risk that traveled around the United States for several years. Another group collected information about *Arabidopsis* plants bred with various genes removed and sent their observations to The Arabidopsis Information Resource (TAIR) for inclusion in its international database of genetic and molecular biology data for the model higher plant *Arabidopsis thaliana*.

We asked the grade 7–16 practitioners to engage in inquiry on two levels, first to design an inquiry experience for their students, then to engage in inquiry themselves by designing and carrying out a research project to investigate the impact of their students' classroom inquiry experience. In the first year of this collaboration, SLCs were responsible for helping each participant develop a Student Inquiry Framework (SIF), a unit using the IT to implement with their classes. In the second year, SLCs helped each participant fine-tune the SIF, then develop a Practitioner Research Plan (PRP) to test the effectiveness of some aspect of it. Each year resulted in a product from each participant. In the first year, it was a reflection on the success of implementation of the SIF. In the second year, participants reported the results of their PRP. (See Chapters 4 and 5 for discussion of these experiences.)

Involvement in inquiry for the science education faculty consisted of pursuing research questions related to the effects of the SLC experience on participants' science content knowledge, uses of information technology in teaching and learning science, and beliefs related to the nature of science. Graduate students in both science and science education were deeply involved in the collection and analysis of data for these research projects and incorporated these research results into presentations at national conferences for both education and the science disciplines. (More information about the shared research agenda appears in Chapter 6.)

SCIENTISTS' CONTRIBUTIONS TO THE SYNERGISTIC INQUIRY EXPERIENCE

Although each SLC was built around a specific theme (e.g., biodiversity, water quality, landscape ecology, or a molecular view of the environment), the members of each SLC were purposefully chosen to build diversity across expertise in science and teaching. Each of the types of members performed a critical role in the quality of the synergistic inquiry experience. However, in particular, the scientists and science graduate students contributed a unique set of expertise to the SLCs with relation to the use of information technology to translate current scientific inquiry to the classroom.

Though many scientists lack the pedagogical content knowledge necessary to design learning activities appropriate to grade 7–16 school settings, we still wanted them to play a key role in helping practitioners to develop and implement learning environments capable of engaging students in authentic inquiry. The question we wanted to address in our SLCs was: "How can scientists contribute to science education directly through their scientific research?" We found that scientists participating in our learning ecology for developing science leadership could provide a meaningful context for authentic inquiry; could model thinking and reasoning to promote inquiry; and could contribute useful IT-based artifacts related to the inquiry, such as specialized measurement tools and procedures, data sets, models of systems, and simulations.

The following sections outline components that scientists were able to contribute as a result of their scientific research that enhanced the synergistic learning experiences of the SLCs. These components existed in both real and virtual settings, and sometimes in a combination of the two. The grade 7–16 practitioners were then able to use the information provided by these components to support the design and implementation of authentic IT-based inquiry in their classrooms.

Synthesis of Scientific Research and Theory

Scientists base their current work on the prior activities and discoveries in their field and related fields. They thus provided for the members of the SLCs a view of the history of scientific concepts and ideas as they relate to major scientific questions. In addition, the scientists provided a critical examination of the early assumptions underlying the generally accepted conceptual theories, along with the integration of prior scientific results to illustrate current understandings and research needs. For example, the chemical engineer and physicist presenting the background of the development of research in nanoscience emphasized the contradictions between the behaviors of various forces at the macro-, micro-, and nanoscales. Of course, these summaries of the history of a field and background of its research themes did not address the level of scaffolding and support needed by the practitioners to make this information immediately useful in the classroom (Burkhardt & Schoenfeld, 2003). But the information shared *did* provide a better foundation on which the practitioners could build stronger pedagogical content knowledge.

Situated Data Sets

The scientists were also able to help participants place specific science concepts into broader contexts. Because of the diversity of the science faculty in each community, they were able to explicitly show the similarities and differences among different concepts, techniques, or analyses across their disciplines. We also encouraged cross-community work at special retreats. As a result of one of these retreats, an Advanced Placement physics teacher who was a member of the Biodiversity Learning Community was able to situate the concept of biodiversity into her physics course as a study of how different shapes of birds' wings impacted lift during flight. She was able to access on the Internet simulations in which various generic wing shapes could be modified to investigate changes in airflow and lift; she planned an inquiry experience around this simulation in which her students created wing shapes to match those of different birds, made conjectures about relationships to their patterns of flight, and then compared those conjectures to actual data on and videos of each type of bird.

Scientific Knowledge Taxonomies and Cognitive Strands

The practitioners' development of effective instructional materials and authentic learning environments was dependent on the quality of understanding of the taxonomy of scientific/social science knowledge and cognitive strands involved in their topics. The scientists were able to provide taxonomies of content surrounding specific domains or scientific questions, stressing the interdisciplinary nature of the science and social science. In addition, they were able to identify the cognitive strands with which the practitioners' students would need more experience in order to develop the adaptive expertise needed to address authentic, ill-structured problems as intelligent novices (Crawford, Schlager, Toyama, Riel, & Vahey, 2005). For example, in the Sustainable Coastal Margins Learning Community, a geologist and geographer worked together to provide the other members of the community with a detailed outline of the connections among the geologic and geographic aspects of the coastal areas being impacted by human activity. Using Geographic Information Systems representations showing changes over time, the scientists and participants created visual models of these connections for their grade 7–16 students.

Researchable Questions of Interest

The first step toward authentic scientific research is to identify a researchable question of interest (Chinn & Malhotra, 2002; Etheredge & Rudnitsky, 2002). Scientists brought to the SLCs ideas on which the members could build questions of interest. For example, the community built around sustainable coastal margins spent the first few days wrangling with what they thought posed the most critical danger for coastal regions, including extreme weather events, natural erosion, and human-made disasters. The science faculty in the community shared with the group how they might use data from remote-sensing devices and simulations to go about investigating solutions to each of these possible problems. The chemists in another SLC posed scenarios related to critical environmental issues (e.g., pesticide use) and discussed how visualizations and simulations could be used to address these issues at the molecular level.

Authentic IT Tools

The scientists in the SLCs were able to bring to the other members the opportunity to work with information technology tools that allowed authentic, significant questions to be addressed. In the summer on-campus experience, members of the SLCs had access to the scientists' actual laboratory environments, with sophisticated equipment such as electron microscopes and mass spectrometers. However, in their interactions with the practitioners, the scientists soon realized that this equipment was too complex, too expensive, and unavailable for the students in the grade 7–16 classroom. With insight provided by the synergy among the various members of the SLCs, everyone came to a clarifying realization that simpler technology tools could be used to *mimic* the scientists' inquiry experiences in the classroom. The scientists took on the challenge of identifying ways to make the information technology tools more student- and school-friendly in order to bring authentic inquiry into the classroom.

These simpler, but still authentic, information technology tools allowed the practitioners to provide for their students opportunities to create and explore models that were amendable based on the students' manipulations and input within their classroom contexts. For example, a biologist designed a simple interface that allowed students to collect data from videos of actual motion within cell organelles at various scales. A biological engineer provided actual data from remote sensors on rivers throughout the state that participants were able to analyze in various ways through the use of a simple spreadsheet application. The geologists introduced participants in their SLC to a simplified version of global information systems software for analyzing worldwide data with relation to location.

SCIENCE GRADUATE STUDENTS' CONTRIBUTIONS TO THE SYNERGISTIC INQUIRY EXPERIENCE

Graduate students both in the science disciplines and in science education served as catalysts for integration of ideas within the SLCs. Their role was that of the *Campus Resource Person* (CRP), helping the practitioners to build connections between their content work with the scientists and their instructional design work with the science educators. Each SLC included two CRPs who worked with the grade 7–16 practitioners continually to help them develop their SIFs and PRPs. (See Chapter 9 for discussion of the impact of participation on the CRPs.)

In particular, the science graduate students were charged with clarifying the components of the science for the other members of the community as they improved their own skills in communicating their science to the public. Because the learning communities were interdisciplinary across science disciplines as well as across science and education, and because practitioners were concerned about bringing the science to their students, the CRPs had to explain content in their fields in ways that could be widely understood, scrapping unnecessary jargon so that they could focus others on the key concepts and vocabulary of the field. For example, a graduate student in landscape ecology designed an online environment of a school playground in which students could explore the vocabulary related to her field in a context that was familiar to them. The science graduate students were also invaluable in working with the practitioners to locate or design technology tools that could mimic aspects of the scientists' and graduate students' research but that were manageable and affordable for the grade 7–16 classroom environment. In one situation, a graduate student in science education and former high school physics teacher located free software online that could be used to make analyzable videos of physical phenomena often investigated in introductory physics courses. With this software, a student or teacher could make a video of a bouncing ball and import measurements taken directly from the video image into a spreadsheet for data analysis. The graduate student then worked with members from all the SLCs to find other applications for this software, for example, collecting and analyzing data on possible genome-related plant movement.

INFORMATION TECHNOLOGY AS A TOOL TO SUPPORT INQUIRY-BASED SYNERGY

Design of innovative instructional materials for authentic inquiry embedded within effective learning environments is likely dependent on fully utilizing the ability of information technology to provide accessibility to manipulable models, simulations, large data sets, and applications for analyzing large data sets (Kali et al., 2008). In the summer experiences in our SLCs, information technology supported the exploration and learning of science through inquiry in the following ways.

Visualization of Complex Data Sets

From birth, most humans are driven to look for and make sense of patterns. In the large and complex data sets encountered in much of today's scientific research, patterns are not easily observable without some technological assistance. Information technology can be used to produce models, simulations, and other representations of these data sets that can then be manipulated by the observer in order to test hypotheses about various observations. For example, one SLC was studying the interactions between biodiversity and environment. A large database had been created from the 50 years of information in the state insect repository. With appropriate information technology tools that connected population data to time and location to create an image on a map of Texas, participants were able to see this information presented in relation to progressions of time and conditions of climate. These representations could be used to investigate questions such as "Has a local change in temperature over time impacted the biodiversity of butterflies in the area?"

Development of Qualitative and Quantitative Conceptual Models

Information technology can provide opportunities for learners, and scientists, to explore the characteristics and dynamics of complex systems in relatively simple ways. Its use can support the development of predictions by learners and scientists and illustrate the possible implications of the system's behavior. For example, software used by the chemists in the Conservation of Energy Learning Community allowed participants to explore with simulations the impacts of changes in heat from within and outside of a system on the various components of the system in public school settings.

Extension of Human Senses

Information technology allows us to collect data and observations at spatial and temporal scales beyond those accessible with our human capabilities. The information technology, in this case, is often coupled with other instruments such as remote sensors. The members of the SLC interested in animal behavior were able to observe grizzly bears in Alaska and pandas in Wolong, China, over the Internet in real time through access to remote video cameras stationed in these locations. The recorded videos were archived and available to the participants for use in making and testing conjectures such as "How much space do grizzlies put between themselves and other grizzlies when catching fish from the same stream?"

CHARACTERISTICS OF IT THAT SUPPORT INQUIRY-BASED SYNERGY

Although the scientists in each SLC used very different, specific IT tools in their own research, we felt that there might be some general aspects of these tools and the ways they were used in the on-campus experiences that would provide us with insight as to their role in promoting inquiry-based synergy in our IT-based learning ecology. Our analysis of the different types of information technology that were used in the various SLCs identified four characteristics common to the IT tools that were most successful in promoting transfer of current science to the classroom.

One of the most important characteristics of an IT tool used to promote the transfer of current science into the classroom is *relevance to current science.* Although this might seem to be an obvious characteristic, it was enlightening to find to what extent IT tools were actually being used in current science. In an interesting exchange between the leaders of the SLCs, a biological engineer who studied water quality was asked which IT tools she used in her research "in the field." With a surprised look on her face, she responded that she very seldom was "in the field," that the data she used were nearly all from remote sensors accessed through her computer in her office. With this perspective, it became clear to us that simple databases and spreadsheets could be used by students to mimic this type of scientific inquiry.

Another common characteristic of the IT used in the SLCs to transfer current science to the classroom is the promotion of *involvement in new science*. With database software that represented insect populations on a map of Texas based on user-presented queries, students could ask and investigate original questions similar to those that might be asked by an entomologist, such as "Is there any relationship between the change in population and distribution of ticks and fire ants over the past 50 years?" Speculations about causes of any relationship seen could then be followed by designing a research project to investigate the possibility of that cause.

A third common characteristic of the IT used is that it provides *accessibility to complex representations*. For example, visualizations with GIS software were used by several SLCs across a wide variety of topics, including investigation of deep-ocean plumes and changes in coastal margins over time. Other complex representations, such as the path of a bouncing ball or the movement of plants over time, were captured in videos that could be observed many times by students in order to collect and analyze data.

Finally, all the IT tools used in the SLCs to transfer current science into the classroom make it possible for students to identify *connections between representations*. For example, in the Nanoscience Learning Community, slide presentation software was used to compare representations of the motion of a particle in three ways: as a video of the motion as seen through an electron microscope, as an animated drawing of the motion, and as a graph of the motion.

EVIDENCE OF INQUIRY-BASED SYNERGY

Our conjecture was that from the synergy created through the distributed expertise of the members of an IT-based learning ecology model would emerge leaders capable of effectively connecting current science practices and classroom inquiry through the use of information technology. Along with the emergence of new leaders, we expected the emergence of various scholarly activities and products related to research in the use of IT to learn and teach science. The shared experience of the SLCs led to different learning outcomes for each of the roles involved. The scientists, science education researchers, grade 7–16 practitioners, and graduate students in science and science education each gained insights they would not have had if they had been working independently.

Perhaps the most unanticipated outcome of the synergistic inquiry experience was just how much the scientists learned about science education. The scientists who persisted in the 6-year program developed a commitment to supporting new ways of teaching science to pre-college students, as well as bringing new ways of teaching to their own undergraduate classrooms. One geologist, after participating in a demonstration of the use of concept mapping as a type of representation of a cognitive domain, returned the next day with a concept map he had created to represent the content knowledge expectations he had for his introductory geology students, exclaiming, "I've been teaching it all wrong!" Rather than merely serving as the subject-matter experts in their particular fields of science, these scientists reached out into the field of science education to better communicate with practitioners and support them in designing their SIF.

Overall, we found that the SLCs that worked well shared five key features that depended on the participation of the scientists. First, the SLC focused on a compelling question rather than having the members merely absorb science content. Second, the scientists did not stop with the presentation of their own research. Rather, they considered how to transfer this research to the grade 7–16 classroom. Third, the scientists modeled scientific practice, not only conducting investigations with practitioners but also explaining the thinking that guided the actions that were taken. In this way, the synergistic inquiry experience functioned as a cognitive apprenticeship, with the scientist serving as an expert who modeled not only practice but also the thought processes behind it. Fourth, scientists in successful SLCs figured out how to package their research so that it was useful to the practitioners, avoiding the more esoteric aspects of their domain to spend more time focusing on the big ideas and fundamental understandings of their field. Finally, the scientists learned to support the practitioners by figuring out ways the practitioners could use inexpensive, readily available, and easily used information technology tools in their classrooms to mimic what the scientists did with expensive scientific tools. For example, one biologist helped practitioners to replicate his work by designing a way to take time-lapse photographs of plants using a simple apparatus consisting of an inexpensive microscope and digital camera. As students set up the equipment to collect the data to compare the plants that differed by only one gene, monitored the validity of the data collection, and analyzed the resulting photos, they engaged in the same types of thinking that the biologist did, though at a fraction of the time and cost involved in his laboratory.

The science graduate students had to consider their own fields from a different perspective. For example, a geosciences doctoral student on a water-quality team had to think about wetlands from a different perspective in order to assist a mathematics teacher in developing an SIF. A master's student in biology participating in a community built around nanoscience research was required to consider scale on a level she would not have encountered in her coursework. For the science education graduate students, working in an SLC offered them a chance to interact directly with scientists and stay closer to the content than their coursework might have required. It also gave them firsthand experience in designing lessons capable of engaging learners in authentic science.

The practitioners felt very positive about working with the scientists and experiencing firsthand what authentic scientific practice feels like. For example, the members of the Water-Quality Learning Community enjoyed the fieldwork they did after a minor flood to collect samples from a research park to hypothesize about and test what was happening in the local watershed. The practitioners also exhibited a willingness to take these experiences into the classroom in a way that would replicate the excitement of inquiry for their students. For example, a middle school teacher-participant from a school with a large population of students of low socioeconomic status applied for and received a grant to purchase the microscopes and digital cameras necessary for her students to contribute data to The Arabidopsis Information Resource. She also co-authored an article on her PRP related to her students' inquiry experience (Stuessy & Metty, 2007).

Evidence collected over the span of the project suggested that for many of us, this experience will have a lasting impact on the way we practice our professions. The synergistic inquiry experience proved key to the overarching project goal of developing leaders in science education capable of using information technology to make the connection between the practice of scientists and the activities of students in science classes.

REFERENCES

American Association for the Advancement of Science (AAAS). (1990). *Science for all Americans*. New York: Oxford University Press.

American Association for the Advancement of Science (AAAS). (1993). *Benchmarks for science literacy*. New York: Oxford University Press.

Burkhardt, H., & Schoenfeld, A. (2003). Improving educational research: Toward a more useful, more influential, and better-funded enterprise. *Educational Researcher, 32*(9), 3–14.

Chinn, C. A., & Malhotra, B. A. (2002). Epistemologically authentic reasoning in schools: A theoretical framework for evaluating inquiry tasks. *Science Education, 86*, 175–218.

Crawford, V. M., Schlager, M., Toyama, Y., Riel, M., & Vahey, P. (2005, April). *Characterizing adaptive expertise in science teaching*. Paper presented at the annual conference of the American Educational Research Association, Montreal, Canada.

Duschl, R., Schweingruber, H., & Shouse, A. (2007). *Taking science to school: Learning and teaching science in grades K–8*. Washington, DC: National Research Council.

Etheredge, S., & Rudnitsky, A. (2002). *Introducing students to scientific inquiry: How do we know what we know?* Boston: Allyn & Bacon.

Kali, Y., Linn, M. C., & Roseman, J. E. (Eds.). (2008). *Designing coherent science education: Implications for curriculum, instruction, and policy*. New York: Teachers College Press.

Krajcik, J. S., Blumenfeld, P., Marx, R. W., Bass, K. M., Fredricks, J., & Soloway, E. (1998). Middle school students' initial attempts at inquiry in project-based science classrooms. *Journal of the Learning Sciences, 7*(3&4), 313–350.

Krajcik, J., Blumenfeld, B., Marx, R., & Soloway, E. (2000). Instructional, curricular, and technological supports for inquiry in science classrooms. In J. Minstrell & E. Van Zee (Eds.), *Inquiry into inquiry: Science learning and teaching* (pp. 283–315). Washington, DC: American Association for the Advancement of Science Press.

National Research Council (NRC). (1996). *National science education standards: Observe, interact, change, learn.* Washington, DC: National Academy Press.

National Research Council (NRC). (2007). *Taking science to school: Learning and teaching science in grades K–8.* Washington, DC: National Academy Press.

Stuessy, C. L., & Metty, J. (2007). The learning research cycle: Bridging research and practice. *Journal of Science Teacher Education, 18*(5), 725–750.

CHAPTER 4

Creating Synergy Through Integrated Professional Development

Carol Stuessy and Stephanie L. Knight

The following quotation captures the reflections of a middle school science teacher who was a member of a Science Learning Community (SLC) in the Information Technology in Science (ITS) Learning Ecology as she engaged in authentic scientific research experiences that required her to master new technology and techniques to seek answers to questions about the genetics of a small mustard plant:

> The intimidation and uncertainty of the unknown or unfamiliar that so often prevents a teacher from implementing something new was not an issue. After repeated use of the technology and data analysis techniques, I became something of an expert. I believe more than anything else, these experiences empowered me to take what I was learning from the research and directly put it into practice in my own classroom. (Stuessy & Metty, 2007, p. 734)

This teacher joined an SLC of other practitioners, graduate students, and plant geneticists to investigate variations in *Arabidopsis thaliana* produced when specific genes were knocked out or when they were grown in different environments. Her learning community produced high-quality visual data with the use of inexpensive digital imaging technologies to reveal differences between wild-type and knock-out mutants, differences that indicated the effects of knocking out a single gene on developmental and physiological phenotypic expressions. The visual data her SLC produced was shared with the broader scientific community through databases and CDs (Plants-In-Motion CD, American Society of Plant Biology, http://www.aspb.org). The community also established a database for classroom use by its members that contained a series of time-lapse video examples and instructional videos for growing *Arabidopsis* and setting up time-lapse video (see http://griffing.tamu.edu). This example is a result of the integrated professional development experiences supported by the ITS Learning Ecology: experiences that brought together scientists, university science educators, graduate students in both science and education, and practitioners in communities to develop new strategies for the use of information technology (IT) to enhance science learning in grade 7–16 classrooms.

INTEGRATED PROFESSIONAL DEVELOPMENT MODEL

The Integrated Professional Development Model (IPDM) emerged as the professional learning and leadership model within the ITS Learning Ecology (see Chapter 1). Participants brought contributions from their own perspectives to develop communities of distributed expertise, playing roles as both learners and teachers in the unique environment that investigated the various ways that information technology is used in doing, teaching, and learning science.

With the support of the diverse members of the ITS Learning Ecology, practitioners enhanced their classroom practice through the design, implementation, and investigation of authentic science lessons. Student Inquiry Frameworks (SIFs) (Stuessy, 2003) incorporated the use of information technology and scientific inquiry to enhance science learners' understanding of the natural world in the same way that scientists use these tools to do their research. Practitioners participating in the ITS Learning Ecology tested their inquiry frameworks in more than 150 classrooms. Many of these same practitioners adapted and used their SIFs as instructional interventions in their own classroom research studies, following a Practitioner Research Plan (PRP) developed by Knight (Knight & Boudah, 2003) to examine the effects of their inquiry frameworks on their own students' learning. Figure 4.1 illustrates the relationships among processes and products of the IPDM.

All participants learned about scientific research as a result of their synergistic inquiry experiences in the SLCs. They learned about innovative practice by applying principles of the learning sciences in the design and testing of their SIFs. They learned to use research methodologies to investigate teaching and learning, to increase their understanding of their own teaching practices, and to improve their own pedagogical content knowledge in science (Feldman & Minstrell, 2000). As a result, the IPDM tightly connects (1) *university coursework* with scientists and university education faculty, (2) *classroom practice* that focuses on the incorporation of information technology and scientific inquiry in grade 7–16 science classrooms, and (3) *practitioner research* initiated and executed by practitioners, graduate students, and university faculty members who want to know more about the effects of information technology and inquiry on

Figure 4.1. Products and Processes of the Integrated Professional Development Model

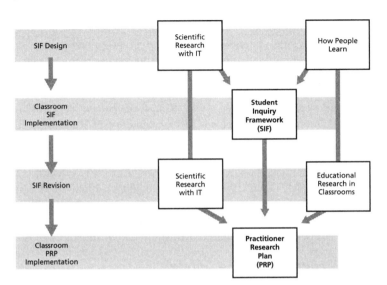

student learning. In this chapter, we focus on the features of the IPDM that progressively emerged from the ITS Learning Ecology and the impact these features had on participants.

The essential features of the IPDM survived 6 years of testing and revision, embedded within a model of progressive refinement. The essential features of the IPDM that are described in this chapter include the following:

- The theoretical basis derived from foundations in cognition, instruction, and assessment embedded within a problem-based design of instruction integrating inquiry and information technology
- Rich scientific research experiences using information technology for all participants
- A two-stage process connecting classroom research to innovative practices in classroom science teaching
- The use of technology in the form of a community portal that connects and organizes interactions between and among ITS Learning Ecology participants
- Enhanced graduate student experiences to prepare for a vision of future leadership in science education

Theoretical Basis of the IPDM

Current research and theory on science teaching and learning influenced development and ongoing revision of the IPDM. Aspects of the model drawn from research include (1) embedding and integrating practitioners' authentic science learning experiences using information technology (e.g., Jacobson & Kozma, 2000; Krajcik et al., 1998; Pellegrino, 2000); (2) challenging practitioners to use authentic scientific inquiry models of pedagogy in their own classroom settings (e.g., Bonnstetter, 1998; Bransford, Brown, & Cocking, 2000; Chinn & Malhotra, 2002; Edelson, 1998; Etheredge & Rudnitsky, 2003); (3) supporting practitioners as they design and explore their own customized classroom implementations of their authentic scientific inquiry experiences (e.g., Kali, Linn, & Roseman, 2008; Krajcik et al., 1998; Linn & Eylon, 2011; Mundry, 2003; Wiggins & McTighe, 1998); and (4) providing a venue for disseminating more formalized classroom-based practitioner research activities investigating the student outcomes associated with the use of IT-mediated authentic scientific inquiry experiences (e.g., Feldman & Minstrell, 2000; Minstrell, 2000).

Design Process for the Model

Brown (1992) described design study as a way to combine research and development in which the investigator must

> tease apart the major features of enticing learning environments: the role of teachers, students, and researchers; the actual contribution of curricula and computer support; methods by which distributed expertise and shared meaning are engineered, and so forth. (p. 174)

Design study provided an excellent method for shaping and adapting the scaffolded experiences for the practitioners, to help them develop methods and strategies for increasing scientific authenticity in their classrooms. The IPDM is, in effect, a "design artifact" (Kelly, 2004, p. 116) that has consolidated "activities, structures, institutions, scaffolds, and curricula" (Design-Based Research Collective, 2003, p. 6). Formative evaluation activities of the first and second stages of maturity in a design study (the planned program and the trial program, as described by Ruiz-Primo, Shavelson, and Baxter [1995]) associated with the processes and products in Figure 4.1 led to the third stage, the development of the prototype IPDM.

The IPDM can be characterized as a seamless continuum of prolonged engagement in professional development. During this engagement, practitioners enhance their pedagogical content knowledge—the content knowledge that deals with the teaching process, including the most useful forms of representing and communicating content and how students best learn the specific concepts and topics of a subject (Shulman, 1986) as it relates to the use of information technology in doing, learning, and teaching science.

The development of the IPDM was informed by a continuous process of review, reflection, and revision, where the following occurred:

1. Major concerns expressed by members of the ITS Learning Ecology were addressed.
2. Different instructional models were employed by instructional teams to enhance practitioners' experiences at the university and inform their own follow-up implementation.
3. Activities, curricula, and other scaffolds were fitted together to create a coherent, tightly connected model of leadership development learning experiences that logically flowed from one experience to another.

Significant revisions occurred as a result of the process. As we realized that the content and strategies needed to be highly differentiated and individualized for participants and that we needed to model the kinds of classroom processes we were advocating for grade 7–16 instruction, the experiences for participants changed dramatically. For example, the summer experiences changed from large-group coursework in the first cohort to small-group interaction in the second cohort, focused around the research topics in the different SLCs. In addition, the Campus Resource Persons (CRPs) available in the second and third cohorts took on responsibilities for providing additional support for and feedback to the participants in the design of their SIFs and PRPs.

Goals for Professional Development

A sequence of experiences was designed to enhance participants' understanding of the role of information technology in doing, teaching, and learning science. By the end of the ITS Learning Ecology experience, we hoped that participants would be able to explain how educational theory and research about how people learn can drive teachers' decision making about the design of an inquiry-based, information technology–rich learning experience for their students. We also expected participants to understand that inquiry-based teaching and learning could achieve varying degrees of scientific authenticity in the classroom and that an assessment plan centered on conceptual understanding and applied through a process of backward design (Wiggins & McTighe, 1998) could assist teachers in deciding what is important for students to learn and be able to do. We also strove to link the focus on inquiry-based learning environments to participants' experiences in their SLCs. We hoped the linkage would be accomplished as participants became more familiar with how their SLCs operated and how similar experiences could be designed for students to increase their knowledge of science, the scientific process, the use of information technology, and related real-world problems and issues.

Professional Development Experiences

Figure 4.2 provides a more detailed schematic of the model as it was developed over the 6 years of the ITS Learning Ecology. Participants engaged in intense experiences in SLCs with scientists in their laboratories, using IT to seek answers to scientific questions during the first professional development institute (Ia). Participants concurrently adapted their authentic research experiences to design similar IT-based research experiences for their students, with the assistance of science educators (IIa) and graduate student mentors (CRPs) (IIb) who were trained prior to the institute in mentoring and the fundamentals of reform-based science teaching and learning (e.g., Bransford et al., 2000).

At the end of the first institute, participants left with an SIF to integrate into their classroom instruction (III). Each SIF included a description of the student population and the context of implementation. Along with the outline of the inquiry experience, the SIF also described suggested evidences of understanding, desired results, and expected challenges or barriers to implementation. Participants were required to share the results of their implementation efforts in order to participate in the second institute. While participants were implementing their SIFs, training in mentoring and fundamentals of educational research occurred for graduate students (IVb) who were chosen to work as CRPs during the professional development activities for the second institute (IVa). During the second institute, participants continued their work with scientists (IVb) and worked with educational researchers (IVa) to design classroom-based PRPs. (A sample SIF can be found in Figure 4.3 and a sample PRP in Figure 5.1.)

PRPs were designed to examine the effects of the refined SIF on students' learning. Participants then implemented their PRPs in their classrooms (V) and had the option of reporting the results of their classroom research during a conference attended by ITS Learning Ecology participants (VI). Multiple and continuous opportunities for discourse and feedback, provided face-to-face in the institutes and electronically via a community portal throughout the entire cycle (VII), were critical to the entire integrated professional development experience.

While the institutes occurred in the initial project during two 3-week periods over two summers, with implementation of the SIF and PRP in the school years between summers, other configurations, including distribution of activities throughout a semester or school year, may work equally well. The critical elements of the professional development involve extensive participation in SLCs that focus on the integration of authentic science research into classroom contexts; time and place for development, implementation, and evaluation of the

Figure 4.2. Detailed Components of the Integrated Professional Development Model

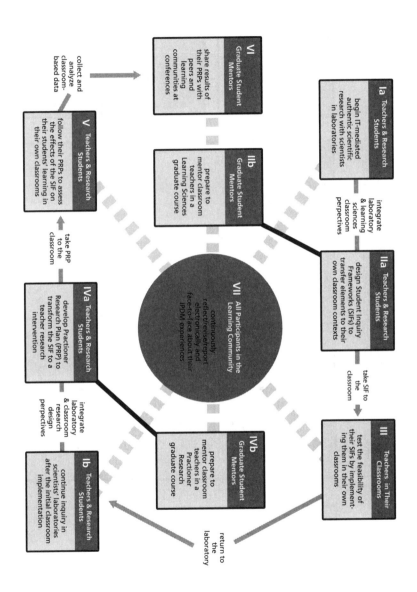

Figure 4.3. Sample Student Inquiry Framework

OBSERVING PLANT RESPONSES USING TIME-LAPSE MOVIE
DAWOON YOO
TEXAS A&M UNIVERSITY

STUDENTS WILL USE TIME-LAPSE MOVIE AND MACRO IMAGING TECHNIQUE TO INVESTIGATE THE DYNAMIC NATURE OF PLANTS

Introduction

- The students' understanding about the natural world could be enhanced by incorporating IT into the science classrooms.
- Students will use time-lapse movie to understand the relationship between stimuli and plant responses.

Students & Context

- 7th-grade students
- Navasota Junior High School
- Life science course
- Possible misconceptions:
  - Plants are not dynamic.
  - Plants don't have hormones.

The Intervention

- Immersion Experience →
  - Students will explore both camera and plant by taking pictures or movies of plants. Students will watch the movies showing "plants in motion."

- HSL Perspectives →
  - Community-centered, knowledge-centered, assessment-centered, and learner-centered learning environment would be promoted.

- Student Research →
  - Using digital camera, students will investigate various plant responses caused by different stimuli.

- Consequential Task →
  - Students will present their movie showing plant responses with detailed explanation.

- Benchmark Experiences/Standards →
  - Digital camera, growing *Arabidopsis*

- Details of Inquiry Sequence →
  - 8 classes in 3 weeks
  - Concept map as a pre-/post-test
  - Final presentation (both formative and summative)

- Scientists' Lab →
  - Digital camera as a research tool
  - *Arabidopsis* as a model organism

Desired Results

- Identifying the relationship between a stimulus and plant response
- Understanding about the investigative nature of scientific enterprise

Evidence of Understanding

- Concept map
- Final presentation including time-lapse movie

Challenges/Barriers

- Use of computers and projector in classrooms
- Growing *Arabidopsis* in classrooms
- Time limitation

impact of student inquiry; and opportunities spaced throughout the process for reflection and discussion with diverse participants within an ITS Learning Ecology environment. As long as these elements are in place, the actual timing or configuration of their occurrence may not be as important. In the sample illustration shown in Figure 4.2, graduate students served as mentors for practitioners and the result was enhanced learning and leadership qualities among the graduate students as well as increased learning by practitioners. However, this approach might work equally well using science coordinators or lead teachers in schools or school districts that are seeking to build local capacity for science leadership.

Technology as Facilitator for Professional Development Experiences

Technology use was at the center of professional development in two ways. The first emphasis was on the use of information technology in the research of scientists and the participation by practitioners with scientists in authentic IT-based research. This use of technology constituted the rich science inquiry experience discussed in Chapters 3 and 8 as a major component of the professional development.

In addition, technology in the form of a community portal was also used as a means to connect and organize interactions within and between groups. The portal supported scientists, graduate students, and practitioners, providing user-friendly opportunities for the development of synergistic relationships that balance face-to-face and electronic formal and informal meetings. An exceptionally user-friendly platform was used to customize specialized tools through design templates for home pages and sub-webs, each of which held document libraries, lists, surveys, announcements, calendars, links, and asynchronous discussion lists. The portal became a primary communication network for participants and provided the interface for summer institutes and courses, follow-up school year surveys, management team information, and focused research webs for subgroups working on particular projects. Periodic surveys requested formative evaluation information that was easily tallied and imported into a database for analysis to assess participants' learning needs and obtain updates on the progress of implementating SIFs and PRPs.

LESSONS LEARNED

After three cohorts of ITS Learning Ecology participation utilizing the IPDM, we learned three critical lessons about the development of leaders in science education who can explain and use information technology in their work as they do, teach, and learn science. These lessons relate to participants' involvement in inquiry through situated uses of information technology, their changes in beliefs about learning and teaching science, and their overall professional growth.

Focused Inquiry with Situated Information Technology

First of all, we learned that information technology situated in a context of scientific inquiry provides an authentic focus for professional development activities for diverse participants to explore new approaches to teaching and learning science. Scientific research experiences involving imaging, modeling, simulation, and manipulation of complex data sets grounded the professional learning supported by the ITS Learning Ecology (see Table 1.1). Edelson (1998) outlined protocols for the research and development of strategies to adapt authentic scientific practice for the classroom, presenting a strong rationale for making science learning more like scientific practice by encouraging attitudes of uncertainty and commitment, including the use of accepted tools and techniques, and establishing a community of sharing. He outlined potential benefits by pointing out that "students become active learners, they acquire scientific knowledge in a meaningful context, and they develop styles of inquiry and communication that will help them to be effective learners" (p. 317). Based on their own personal experiences with IT-based inquiry in the SLCs, participants used Edelson's guidelines in the development of the SIF. The SIF was the vehicle for communicating ideas about transforming authentic laboratory research to classroom settings; new visions of classroom inquiry and assessment for conceptual understanding; and work with scientists to transport, build, and/or modify the information technology used in the laboratory to make it appropriate for classroom use.

Change in Conceptual Models of Learning and Teaching

Second, we learned that teaching by inquiry with information technology requires professional development that enables practitioners to actively change their conceptual models of how science is learned and taught. Design of instruction modeling the use of information technology in doing authentic scientific inquiry is impacted by how practitioners think about their students' learning and, consequently, about their own teaching (Edelson, 1998; Krajcik et al., 1998; Mundry, 2003). We knew from pre-institute surveys that participants in the ITS Learning Ecology were not very familiar with inquiry teaching strategies based on information technology. Scientific inquiry presupposes instruction that supports student-directed learning (National Research Council, 1996). Universally, science educators continue to affirm the significant and unique contributions of student-directed discovery as the most effective way to learn about the natural world (National Research Council, 2007). Embedded assessment methods should make students' thinking visible throughout the inquiry process, and appropriate inquiry instruction includes attention to supporting scientific habits of mind, such as how to use evidence to support knowledge claims about how the world works (Sandoval & Millwood, 2005). Effective inquiry learning environments support practices that include collaboration, argumentation, reflection, revision, and peer assessment (Goldman, Petrosino, & The Cognition and Technology Group at Vanderbilt, 1999; Petrosino, 2003). To impact the science classrooms of our practitioners, we had to help participants resolve their beliefs and practices of teaching and learning with the idea that inquiry facilitated through the use of IT is indeed a viable method for their own classrooms of learners. As Mundry (2003) tells us, dissonance-creating and dissonance-resolving experiences need to be directly connected to practitioners' own contexts. "They need to have direct experience seeing how the method works with their own students, [and] until teachers are supported to try out inquiry with their own students, they are unlikely to transform their thinking" (Mundry, 2003, p. 129). Therefore, we required all participants to implement what they had learned in their SLC experience in their own classrooms, with the expectation that their learning communities would help them identify ways to address any constraints of time, administrative policies, technology access, and standardized testing pressures that they encountered.

Professional Growth Through Integrated Professional Development

Finally, we learned that integrated professional development based on synergistic inquiry experiences within heterogeneous SLCs can take all participants to new levels of learning and leadership. Through their work in the ITS Learning Ecology, individuals from the various populations involved became leaders in their respective universities, secondary schools, community colleges, and professional organizations. For example, future trajectories for many practitioners changed to include part-time and full-time graduate work toward advanced degrees in both science and education. Practitioners who enrolled in graduate programs engaged in collaborations with their mentor scientists to complete theses and dissertations reflecting the vision of the ITS Learning Ecology. Graduate students in science and in education began to envision professional futures that included goals in both education and science. For example, pairs of graduate student mentors consisting of one science graduate student and one science education graduate student facilitated small-group interaction and became liaisons between faculty in science and education so that the two populations became better integrated. (See Chapter 9 for additional description of the impact of the experience on both science and science education graduate students.) Faculty members in education supported both science and education graduate students in their liaison work by designing and teaching two 3-week intensive graduate-level courses that presented principles of mentoring and educational research methods. As a result of these courses, science and education graduate students developed greater respect for each other's work. Education faculty also expanded their own roles to include collaboration with scientists who now do research on science teaching and learning in a number of venues, including university undergraduate classrooms. Faculty members in the sciences became leaders in their own communities who now speak for outreach and involvement in grade 7–16 education with the authority of firsthand experience in working with public school teachers and educational researchers. In general, the integration of the diverse populations within the components of the Integrated Professional Development Model resulted in the development of a variety of new leaders in science education.

REFERENCES

Bransford, J., Brown, A., & Cocking, R. (Eds.) (2000). *How people learn: Brain, mind, experience, and school* (expanded ed.). Washington, DC: National Academy Press.

Brown, A. L. (1992). Design experiments: Theoretical and methodological challenges in creating complex interventions in classroom settings. *Journal of the Learning Sciences,* 2(2), 141–178.

Bonnstetter, R. J. (1998). Inquiry: Learning from the past with an eye on the future. *Electronic Journal of Science Education,* 3(1). Retrieved February 10, 2012, from http://unr.edu/homepage/jcannon/ejse/bonnstetter.html.

Chinn, C. A., & Malhotra, B. A. (2002). Epistemologically authentic inquiry in schools: A theoretical framework for evaluating inquiry tasks. *Science Education,* 86(2), 175–218.

Design-Based Research Collective. (2003). Design-based research: An emerging paradigm for educational inquiry. *Educational Researcher,* 32(1), 5–8.

Edelson, D. (1998). Realising authentic science learning through the adaptation of science practice. In G. J. Fraser & K. Tobin (Eds.), *International handbook of science education, Vol. 2* (pp. 317–331). Dordrecht, Netherlands: Kluwer.

Etheredge, S., & Rudnitsky, A. (2003). *Introducing students to scientific inquiry: How do we know what we know?* Boston: Pearson Education.

Feldman, A., & Minstrell, J. (2000). Action research as a research methodology in the study of the teaching and learning of science. In E. Kelly & R. Lesh (Eds.), *Handbook of research design in mathematics and science education* (pp. 429–456). Mahwah, NJ: Lawrence Erlbaum Associates.

Goldman, S. R., Petrosino, A. J., & The Cognition and Technology Group at Vanderbilt. (1999). Design principles for instruction in content domains: Lessons from research on expertise, learning. In F. T. Durso, R. S., Nicherson, R. W. Schvaneveldt, S. T. Dumais, D. S. Lindsay, & M. T. H. Chi (Eds.), *Handbook of applied cognition* (pp. 595–627). New York: Wiley.

Jacobson, M. J., & Kozma, R. B. (Eds.). (2000). *Innovations in science and mathematics education: Advanced designs for technologies of learning.* Mahwah, NJ: Lawrence Erlbaum Associates.

Kali, Y., Linn, M., & Roseman, J. E. (2008). *Designing coherent science education: Implications for curriculum, instruction, and policy.* New York: Teachers College Press.

Kelly, A. (2004). Design research in education: Yes, but is it methodological? *Journal of the Learning Sciences, 13,* 115–128.

Knight, S. (2003, April). *Using action research to bridge the gap between science and educational research.* Paper presented at the annual meeting of the American Educational Research Association, Chicago.

Knight, S., & Boudah, D. (2003) Participatory research and development. In D. Wiseman & S. Knight (Eds.), *The impact of school-university collaboration on K-12 student outcomes* (pp. 181–195). Washington, DC: American Association of Colleges of Teacher Education.

Krajcik, J., Phyllis, P. C., Marx, R. W., Bass, K. M., Fredricks, J., & Soloway, E. (1998). Inquiry in project-based science classrooms: Initial attempts by middle school students, *Journal of the Learning Sciences, 7*(3&4), 313–350.

Linn, M., & Eylon, B. (2011). *Science learning and instruction: Taking advantage of technology to promote knowledge integration.* New York: Routledge.

Minstrell, J. (2000). Implications for teaching and learning inquiry. In J. Minstrell & E. H. van Zee (Eds.), *Inquiring into inquiry learning and teaching in science* (pp. 471–496). Washington, DC: American Association for the Advancement of Science.

Mundry, S. (2003). Honoring adult learners: Adult learning theories and implications for professional development. In J. Rhoton & P. Bowers (Eds.), *Science teacher retention: Mentoring and renewal* (pp. 123–132). Arlington, VA: NSTA Press.

National Research Council. (1996). *National science education standards.* Washington, DC: National Academy Press.

National Research Council. (2007). *Taking science to school: Learning and teaching science in grades K–8.* Washington, DC: National Academy Press.

Pellegrino, J. W. (2000). Leveraging the power of learning theory through information technology. In American Association of Colleges of Teacher Education (Ed.), *Log on or lose out: Technology in the 21st century* (pp. 48–54). Washington, DC: American Association of Colleges of Teacher Education.

Petrosino A. J. (2003). Commentary: A framework for supporting learning and teaching about mathematical and scientific models. *Contemporary Issues in Teacher and Teacher Education, 3*(3), 288–299.

Ruiz-Primo, M. A., Shavelson, R. J., & Baxter, J. P. (1995). Evaluation of a prototype teacher enhancement program on science performance assessment. In P. Kansanen (Ed.), *Discussion on some education issues* (Vol. 1, pp. 171–200). Helsinki, Finland: Department of Teacher Education.

Sandoval, W. A., & Millwood, K. A. (2005). The quality of students' use of evidence in written scientific explanations. *Cognition and Instruction, 23,* 23–55.

Shulman, L. S. (1986). Those who understand: Knowledge growth in teaching. *Educational Researcher, 15*(2), 4–14.

Stuessy, C. L. (2003). *Instructional framework (IF) templates.* Class hand-out for EDCI 689, Summer 2003. College Station: Texas A&M University.

Stuessy, C. L., & Metty, J. S. (2007). The learning research cycle: Bridging research and practice. *Journal of Science Teacher Education, 18,* 725–750.

Wiggins, G., & McTighe, J. (1998). *Understanding by design.* Alexandria, VA: Association for Supervision and Curriculum Development.

CHAPTER 5

Creating Synergy Through Practitioner Research

Stephanie L. Knight, Carol Stuessy,
and Margaret Hobson

As described in Chapter 1, the purpose of the Information Technology in Science (ITS) Learning Ecology was to provide an environment for productive adaptation and development of a diverse group of participants through the use of information technology (IT) as a vehicle for inquiry. A dual emphasis on inquiry—inquiry in the scientist's laboratory and inquiry into teaching and learning—provided the common basis for collaboration among the rather disparate populations represented. This focus required a paradigm shift in teaching and learning from teacher-centered to student-centered instruction. This shift placed tremendous pressure on practitioners to provide the kinds of instruction and assessment that foster student engagement and independence during inquiry activities. In addition, scientists and science educators were required to forge connections between their teaching and research (see, e.g., Blumenfeld, Kempler, & Krajcik, 2006; Bransford, Brown, & Cocking, 1999, 2000). Research on instructional implementation conducted by practitioners in their own settings provided a structure for the understanding and unification of the different roles and enabled participants to cross traditional boundaries of research and practice.

A number of different terms can be used to refer to classroom research: practitioner inquiry (Cochran-Smith & Lytle, 2004), practitioner research, action research (Zeichner & Noffke, 2001), teacher research (Cochran-Smith & Lytle, 1999), self-study (Cole & Knowles, 2001), and scholarship of teaching and learning (Shulman, 2000). While the various terms are slightly different, they share common features such as the practitioner as researcher, the professional context as the research site, and blurred boundaries between research and practice (Cochran-Smith & Donnell, 2006). By whatever label, practitioner research, which embodies collaboration and reflection focused on a teacher's own practice, provides a vehicle for effective professional development (Freedman, 2001).

When viewed as professional development, the goal of practitioner research is to link research with practice in order to impact practitioner thinking and instructional behavior, institutional systems and culture, and student outcomes. In particular, the participation in communities of practice focused on improvement of teaching and learning through practitioner research may bring about positive change (Richardson & Placier, 2001). While these communities of practice have traditionally involved teachers, other stakeholders in student learning outside of the school setting may be important to include (Hargreaves, 2003). In the case of the ITS Learning Ecology, science and education faculty, researchers, and graduate students in both science and education collaborated with practitioners to improve and study student learning in grades 7–16.

In contrast to professional development within learning communities, many types of staff development have experienced little success in effecting lasting change, perhaps because teachers often see little relation between their needs and the in-service opportunities provided (Richardson & Placier, 2001). Staff development often lacks authenticity from the perspective of teachers who are primarily concerned about student learning in their own classrooms. Practitioner research, on the other hand, provides more authentic professional development because teachers can evaluate the immediate impact of their professional development on students. Some support for its potential to add to the knowledge base on teaching and learning has also recently emerged (Cochran-Smith & Donnell, 2006). In particular, practitioner research is credited with building local knowledge that other teachers can use to improve classroom practice (Lytle & Cochran-Smith, 1994; Cochran-Smith & Donnell, 2006).

Practitioner research within the ITS Learning Ecology served three major purposes:

1. Authentic professional development for practitioners
2. The means to measure the added value of participation in IT-based inquiry for its impact on students of practitioners who were participants
3. Focus on the common goal of developing practitioner research to unite the diverse participants into a community of practice

This chapter provides a description of the process and impact of using practitioner research to work toward these three purposes.

PRACTITIONER RESEARCH AS AUTHENTIC PROFESSIONAL DEVELOPMENT

One assumption of the ITS Learning Ecology was that science teaching and learning at grades 7–16 will be improved when practitioners in these settings become more connected to the IT-based authentic science research done in field settings or laboratories and engage in practitioner research to investigate the impact of applying authentic inquiry to their own classrooms. The ITS Learning Ecology practitioner research experience, as part of the Integrated Professional Development Model (IPDM), involved all three types of inquiry delineated by Anderson and Helms (2001), including inquiry as a descriptor of scientific research, inquiry as a mode of student learning, and inquiry as a type of teaching. Creating the Practitioner Research Plan (PRP) included three phases of implementation corresponding to the three types of inquiry:

1. Practitioner involvement with university faculty in science research using IT
2. Translation of the authentic science research experience into authentic experiences for students in their classrooms
3. Development and implementation of a PRP to determine the impact of the use of IT to improve student learning

In the course of the design experiment described in Chapter 4, several features were identified and refined to optimize the use of practitioner research as professional development.

Features of the Practitioner Research Plan

The original model or blueprint for the classroom research used in the ITS Learning Ecology context, called Participatory Research and Development (PR&D), was funded by the U.S. Department of Education, Office of Special Education Programs to focus on bridging the gap between research and practice (Knight & Boudah, 2003). The goal was to develop and implement a research and development model that would build a learning community within secondary schools and, specifically, impact teacher thinking and instructional behaviors, the performance of students, and the climate of school systems. Results of the 4-year project indicated that teachers provided more interactive instruction and discussion and that students were engaged in more learning strategy–related activities and exhibited fewer off-task behaviors (Knight & Boudah, 2003). In addition, teachers began to see the link between research and teaching and became more cognizant of the needs and abilities of low-achieving students and those with disabilities (Boudah & Knight, 1999).

Since the goals of teacher professional development and community building were similar in that project and the ITS Learning Ecology, we adapted the PR&D blueprint for use with ITS practitioners. Each time practitioners in the various cohorts of the ITS Learning Ecology implemented the PRPs, a cycle of evaluation, feedback, and reflection by all those involved occurred before, during, and after the implementation, resulting in changes to the components. The following sections outline the features of the PRP that emerged from the cycles as necessary for the success of the integrated professional development experience for participants. Figure 5.1 provides a sample PRP produced by a practitioner.

Figure 5.1. Sample Practitioner Research Plan (Page 1)

Dynamic Osmosis:
A comparison of the effects of static modeling compared to dynamic modeling in the study of osmosis on student understanding and knowledge transfer.

By: Sandra Metoyer

Texas A&M University

ITS Center for Teaching and Learning

Abstract:

Knowledge transfer is a persistent concern in educational research. It is important for individuals involved in education to examine their methods and ask themselves to what extent the knowledge gained by their students is *transferred* to similar but new circumstances and examples.

The question explored here is how to teach in a method, progression, and style that not only enables students to learn a difficult concept, but also facilitates knowledge transfer.

I have chosen to use the concept of osmosis as a test topic for this framework. The "first and only goal" of teaching is long-term retention and transfer (Halpern, 2003). In the specific example of osmosis, the ability to visualize this concept at the particulate level may lead to a better understanding of other chemical and biological processes.

Research Questions:

Research indicates there is an increase in understanding and transfer when a concept is presented in multiple, altered and varied contexts.

1. How much does each new context improve understanding and transfer of the concept?

A dynamic model where students can see the constant random movement of molecules may allow them to create a more realistic mental model of the concept .This, in turn, may improve their ability to transfer new knowledge to unfamiliar examples and contexts.

2. How do computer animations affect level of understanding and transfer with each new context as compared with students that create static models and do not use computer animations?

Increasing Participants' Level of Comfort with Educational Research. Teachers' mistrust and misunderstanding of educational research has been well documented in the literature, and numerous studies document the gap between research and practice and the need to bridge this gap in order to improve teaching and learning (see e.g., Clandinin & Connelly, 1996; Fuchs & Fuchs, 1990).

Figure 5.1. Sample Practitioner Research Plan (Page 2)

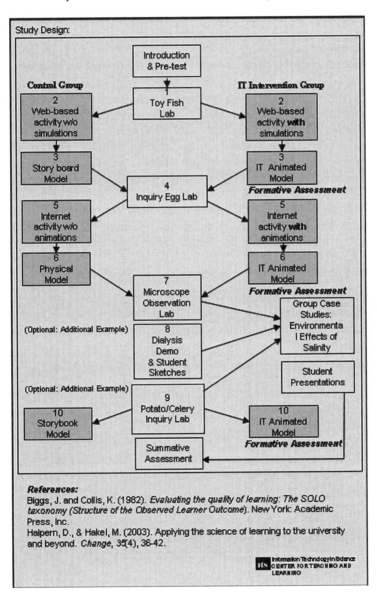

References:
Biggs, J. and Collis, K. (1982). *Evaluating the quality of learning: The SOLO taxonomy (Structure of the Observed Learner Outcome)*. New York: Academic Press, Inc.
Halpern, D., & Hakel, M. (2003). Applying the science of learning to the university and beyond. *Change*, 35(4), 36-42.

Furthermore, even when practitioners are convinced of the value of research for practice, they do not see it as an activity that they can successfully conduct. For this reason, the practitioner research experience needed to convince participants of the value of research and of their own potential for successful participation. While the efforts initially targeted teachers, it became clear as we implemented the practitioner research experience that understanding of practitioner research was not consistent across the various types of participants. Increasing understanding of educational research in general, and practitioner research specifically, needed to be extended to encompass the diverse populations represented in the ITS Learning Ecology.

We used several approaches to increase everyone's level of comfort with the educational research. First, we learned to avoid educational research terminology that was unfamiliar to both practitioners and scientists. We tried to present research on a continuum from less formal to more formal, with less formal approaches being used by practitioners in their everyday work. Practitioners initially engaged in a less formal research experience, recording and discussing their impressions of the impact of piloting their IT-based Student Inquiry Frameworks (SIFs; discussed in Chapter 4) prior to implementing their more formal PRPs.

Providing Support for the Design of Practitioner Research. We scaffolded the more formal PRP through the use of a series of questions that gradually but explicitly led participants through the process step-by-step (see Figure 5.2).

Figure 5.2. Scaffolding for the Practitioner Research Plan

I. Identification of Challenge: What challenge will you address using information technology (IT)? Is this challenge under your control in your setting? Why do you think IT will address the challenge? Is this challenge student-centered?

II. Design of IT Intervention (The Student Inquiry Framework)

    A. *Rationale:* What IT will you use to address the challenge?

       Why do you think this particular technology will address your challenge (experiences in ITS research team, review of prior research)? Is the IT feasible for your classroom or other setting?

    B. *IT Intervention Description:* Who will use the IT? What IT will you or others use? What activities will you use in conjunction or for implementation? What materials/equipment will you need? How will you and/or others use IT? For what purpose will you/they use it? What are your goals and objectives? Where and when will your IT intervention take place? How long will it last?

    C. *Anticipated Outcomes:* What do you expect to happen as a result?

III. Development of Data Collection Plan

A. *Inquiry Questions:* What specific questions will you address? Are your questions specific and clear enough that someone else would know what you are doing? Do they address the challenge you identified? Do they reflect the intervention you are doing? Do they specify the target of the IT intervention? Are they focused on student challenges to learning? What research has been done in a similar area of inquiry and how has it informed your decisions?

B. *Methods:* Who will you collect data from? (Everyone who experienced the intervention? A smaller group?) How were they chosen? Who will assist you with the data collection? What would learners know or do as a result of the IT intervention that would indicate to you (or others) that the intervention had (or had not) made a difference? What data will you collect to determine this? If you obtain these data, will they enable you to answer your questions? How will you obtain the data (steps or procedures, tools, instruments)? How will others help you with your process? When will you collect data (timeline for evaluation)? Why are you using this way to collect data? Are the time and effort needed to collect the data worth the information you will get?

C. *Determination of Analysis, Interpretation, and Dissemination Plan:* What roles will you and others have in the analysis? What kind of data will you get (scores, descriptions, categories)? How do you plan to analyze/display your data so you can see if it answers your questions so you can discuss it with others? How will you convince others that your findings were a result of the intervention? What else might cause these findings and how have you addressed them in your plan?

The design of the PRP included identification of learner-centered challenges, choice of a particular IT-mediated intervention to address the challenge, design of an intervention to measure the effects of the intervention on the challenge, and plans for analysis and display of the data collected. Practitioner research groups formed on the basis of common interests related to a challenge, type of IT, type of intervention, or type of learner. Since participants varied widely in their familiarity and experience with classroom research, a variety of optional workshops on various topics (e.g., Designing Rubrics, Graphical Display of Data) were provided "on demand." Each day, participants chose from a list of topics, or submitted a desired topic, as their needs evolved. Faculty and Campus Resource Persons (CRPs) provided the requested workshops. Interaction among practitioners and professors and graduate student mentors became increasingly individualized as the plans were developed.

Focusing on Student Learning. The major question in the first section of the research plan involved the challenge to student learning that the proposed SIF would address. In particular, why would the proposed experience with information technology make a difference in student learning? We also prompted practitioners through questions to think about whether the challenge was under their control and whether it focused on student learning. Challenges to student learning that involved parents and family or external mandates are not typically under the control of the teacher, but challenges that can be addressed by instruction or classroom environment are manipulable.

The second set of questions focused on the IT intervention itself (the SIF), which had been developed and informally tested in a practitioner's classroom setting, and the procedures for use of the framework in the classroom as part of the research. Practitioners responded to questions prompting them to describe the SIF and their reasons for thinking that it would address the challenge described. Practitioners drew on their experiences implementing the framework in their classrooms as well as other research about the impact of the proposed IT to develop their rationale. One question probed the feasibility for use of the particular IT within the framework and often resulted in collaboration among scientists, educational researchers, and practitioners in adapting or substituting appropriate IT within the classroom. Practitioners soon realized that the IT interventions for the practitioner research and the SIF were the same but that additional, systematic steps were necessary to provide the level of detail and specificity needed for the PRP.

The final set of questions helped the practitioners determine how they would collect data about the impact of the SIF on student learning and consisted of three areas—research questions, methods, and analysis and interpretation. The PRP focused participants on the relationship between the classroom processes in the inquiry framework and student outcomes. For this phase, the CRPs—graduate students in education and science—assisted groups and individuals as they developed their research questions and subjected them to queries about whether their questions addressed the challenge described, whether the questions were related to the IT intervention specified, and whether the questions specifically targeted student learning.

Discussions during development of the research plan often centered around questions such as "What would convince me that the SIF had the desired results?" and "How would I convince others that my student outcomes were a consequence of the SIF?" As a result, the practitioners spent considerable time and effort discussing and devising performance assessments that went beyond the typical multiple-choice or end-of-chapter tests they had used in the past. They scrutinized samples of student work and developed and tested rubrics to capture the processes as well as the products of student inquiry. They realized the importance of embedding assessments within the context of the inquiry so that authenticity was maintained, and they struggled with questions of formative and summative assessment. Most incorporated comparison groups into their research.

The practitioner research experience emphasized several components that focused practitioners on student outcomes. First, practitioners were directed to determine a challenge to student learning in their own classrooms that IT would have the potential to address. Throughout the experience, scientists and science educators emphasized the need for practitioners to translate their research experiences with the Science Learning Community (SLC) into experiences for their students. The PRP was a means of assessing how this translation impacted student learning.

Impact of Practitioner Research on Practitioners

Throughout the process of research within the ITS Learning Ecology, scientists, science educators, and science and education graduate students studied the impact on the practitioners in grades 7–16. Questions about the quality of IT-based SIFs and PRPs, attitudes toward research, the perceived efficacy for implementing research, and the relationships among these variables framed the studies. The following sections summarize the findings from these studies (Hobson, 2009; Knight, 2003; Knight, Pedersen, Vannest, Stuessy, & Ormiston, 2005; Knight, Pedersen, & Morales, 2006; Moseley & Schielack, 2005).

Quality of Practitioner Research Plans. To determine the quality of the PRPs, we constructed the Inquiry Squared Rubric (Knight, Pedersen, Vannest, Stuessy, & Ormiston, 2005), as shown in Table 5.1, to score various components of the plan related to inquiry.

Two types of inquiry were identified: (1) IT-based inquiry that participants designed and incorporated into SIFs used as interventions for the students in their classes, and (2) inquiry focusing on the impact of the SIF on students. Current research and theory about inquiry and representational competence and use by students (e.g., Bonnstetter, 1998; Duschl, 2008; Lehrer & Schauble, 2004; Lesh & Doerr, 2003; Minstrell, 2000) and research quality (NRC, 2000) informed the design of the scoring rubric. For example, the six stages of inquiry specified by Bonnstetter and used in the design of the SIF (see Chapter 4) were incorporated into scoring of the component in the rubric called "Inquiry Type." Other categories included Use of Multiple Representations, Content Outcomes, Nature of Science Outcomes, Argumentation Opportunities for Students, and Representational Fluency Using IT. Initially, the rubric was used to score the SIF planned by the practitioner, not the actual inquiry engaged in by students, which may differ. However, practitioners were able to use the rubric to determine the level of inquiry in which students actually engaged and the gap between intended level and actual level when implemented. In this way, the rubric served as a tool for reflection and instructional improvement.

Table 5.1. Inquiry Squared Rubric

	0	1	2	3
Inquiry 1: Related to the Student Inquiry Framework				
Inquiry Type	None	Teacher-Directed	Shared	Student-Directed
Use of Multiple Representations	None	Illustrative in direct instruction	Question and answer—teacher control of discussion	Students work directly with them
Content Outcomes	None	Rote	Connected facts and concepts	Deep, applied understanding
Nature of Science (NOS) Outcomes	None	Traditional Scientific Method	NOS suggested	NOS very visible
Argumentation Required	None	Superficial	Suggests connection to data	Strong claim
Representational Fluency	None	Mechanical rote replication of IT	Makes connections with extant models	Makes own models—data is queried
Inquiry 2: Related to the Practitioner Research Plan				
Theoretical Framework	None	Incoherent/inconsistent	Coherent but lacks depth	Coherent with depth
Research Questions	None	Neither meaningful nor testable	Either meaningful or testable, not both	Both meaningful and testable
Design	None	Not well matched to research questions/naive	Fairly well matched but missing information	Well matched to research questions and sufficient detail
Participants	None	Specified but not described	Some, but missing important information	Very detailed
Instruments	None	Inappropriate or insufficient	Sufficient but lacking evidence of validity and reliability	Validated and capable of answering questions

Table 5.1. Inquiry Squared Rubric (continued)

	0	1	2	3
Inquiry 2: Related to the Practitioner Research Plan				
Data Analysis	None	Some analysis but serious flaws	Some detail about analysis but somewhat flawed	Appropriate and very detailed
Procedures	None	Inappropriate and/or lacking detail	Appears appropriate but lacks sufficient detail	Both appropriate and detailed
Conclusions	None	Superficial (feelings—no reference to data)	Suggests connections based on data	Makes claims supported by student data

The PRP section of the rubric contained components similar to those specified in Table 5.1, including Theoretical Framework, Research Questions, Design, Participants, Instruments, Data Analysis, and Procedures. Using the PRP headings as guides, we examined PRPs to determine common and divergent elements. Problems related to a deep conceptual understanding of science by students in participants' classes emerged as the challenge to learning most commonly identified as the impetus for the IT intervention, followed by concerns about attitudes toward science and motivation to learn and enjoy science. The type of IT selected as an intervention to address these challenges varied widely, with use of interactive websites, varied modeling and visualization software, and video accompanied by an Excel workbook to enable data collection and analysis used most frequently. The determination of the research design was perhaps the most difficult part of the process for most of the participants.

Perceptions of Value and Confidence in Relation to Practitioner Research. At strategic points, participants completed online surveys to measure their confidence in doing practitioner research. Given that learners construct meaningful understanding of new information based on previous knowledge (Bransford et al., 1999, 2000), design of professional development experiences needs to incorporate the prior knowledge and experiences of participants. In the case of the ITS Learning Ecology, with its primary focus on IT-based inquiry as a vehicle for research as well as for facilitating conceptual understanding, participants' perceptions of their research ability could impact not only current learning and performance but also future use of practitioner research. Participants reported significantly higher readiness for research following the development of their PRPs. However, the considerable variation of individuals in earlier cohorts led to more individualization of learning experiences in subsequent cohorts.

Following completion and submission of their PRPs, participants responded to online questions regarding their perceptions of the value of the experience and their level of confidence for actually implementing their plan. ITS Learning Ecology participants exhibited high levels of satisfaction with the experience and confidence in plan completion. Overall, they indicated that the ITS Learning Ecology experience had met their expectations, and they perceived that the PRP experiences were valuable and that the amount of time spent on the process was "just enough." Finally, when asked about their level of confidence in completing the process in the coming months, participants responded with a high level of confidence. Examination of group differences in perceptions revealed similar positive experiences despite SLC membership or the role played within the ITS Learning Ecology.

We should note here that despite high confidence, practitioners encountered barriers to implementation in their school settings that prevented many from successfully enacting the research. Some practitioners returned to a new curriculum with an inflexible schedule and mandated instructional approaches. A few practitioners discovered that their districts required them to do exactly the same thing in all of their sections, thereby eliminating the possibility of having a control group for their research. Although some practitioners managed to address or overcome the barriers they encountered and implement their research plans, others were not in a position to make the decisions necessary for implementation.

Teacher Leadership as a Result of Practitioner Research. The impact of practitioner research on the teacher leadership of participants in the ITS Learning Ecology was varied. The participants completed the *Teacher Leadership Roles Survey* (Hobson, 2009), which is a combination of two Smylie and Denny (1990) surveys. Results indicated that after participating in practitioner research within the ITS Learning Ecology experience, practitioners' primary leadership roles involved serving as a source of knowledge for teachers and being a generator of new ideas for teachers. Primary activities included development of curricular and instructional materials, attendance at program-related meetings, and engagement in building-level decision making.

PRACTITIONER RESEARCH AS THE CATALYST FOR COMMUNITIES OF PRACTICE

Participation with others in inquiry addresses the social nature of the construction of knowledge and the collective nature of knowing (e.g., Rogoff & Lave, 1984; Vygotsky, 1986). Group interactions create opportunities for learning

(Little, 1993), increase the resources available to individuals, and enable participants to process shared information through communication and collaboration (Rosenholtz, 1989). Since much of teacher knowledge is tacit and based on experience (Kagan, 1990), teachers may not be able to articulate to others their assumptions, beliefs, and understandings in a manner necessary for conscious examination. As individuals interact in groups, they acquire common understandings and language. Group discussion becomes a vehicle for articulating, examining, and changing beliefs (Schecter & Parkhurst, 1993). Beliefs, in turn, strongly influence behavior (Bandura, 1986). While beliefs have traditionally been resistant to change, some evidence exists that the combination of collaboration and reflection over a period of years impacts both beliefs and practices (Richardson & Placier, 2001). Discourse communities or *communities of practice* emerge as means of acquiring cognitive tools to make sense of situations and understand various perspectives, appropriating expertise, and developing insights about the nature of teaching and learning (Putnam & Borko, 2000). Richardson and Placier (2001) note that "long term collaborative, and inquiry oriented programs with in-service teachers appear to be quite successful in changing beliefs, conceptions, and practices" (p. 921). Participation in communities of practice focused on improvement of teaching and learning may bring about positive changes in the beliefs and practices of participants (Richardson & Placier, 2001). The collaborative research groups based on shared research interests in the ITS Learning Ecology served as communities of practice that impacted participants' beliefs and behaviors.

Community-Based Features of the Practitioner Research Plan

Graduate students who functioned as CRPs served as brokers or liaisons for the collaboration of scientists, education researchers, and practitioners. They typically worked in pairs consisting of one education graduate student and one science graduate student with groups of practitioners who had self-selected into groups based on common interests. In this way, the paired graduate students could address science content, technology, and education research questions with their practitioner groups. They also enlisted the assistance of various groups as they worked through the questions in the PRP that required the expertise of all involved.

Graduate student pairs met with education researchers and scientists on a regular basis to discuss progress of the PRPs, specific needs of practitioners, and their own needs as mentors. The opportunity for joint reflection and the forming and re-forming of structures and support provided by education and science researchers based on their feedback and reflection resulted in enhanced professional development for all.

Impact of Practitioner Research on Communities of Practice

During the stage of determining research questions and data collection methods, science researchers and graduate students began to see similarities between the science research they conducted and the social science research required for the PRP. Many formal and informal discussions comparing methods and instruments took place between scientists and educators during this period (see Chapter 8). Respect for the different areas of expertise that each group brought to bear on the task of developing research plans emerged, and roles began to merge as each group gained expertise from the other. Recognition of similarity in research paradigms, realization of differences between science and social science research, and respect for distributed expertise became a catalyst for collaboration in ITS Learning Ecology research as well as in future science learning research opportunities.

REFERENCES

Anderson, R., & Helms, J. (2001). The ideal of standards and the reality of schools: What research says about inquiry. *Journal of Research in Science Teaching* 38(1), 3–16.

Bandura, A. (1986). The explanatory and predictive scope of self-efficacy theory. *Journal of Social and Clinical Psychology* 4, 359–373.

Blumenfeld, P. C., Kempler, T. M., & Krajcik. J. S., (2006). Motivation and cognitive engagement in learning environments. In R. K. Sawyer (Ed.), *Cambridge Handbook of the Learning Sciences* (pp. 475–488). New York: Cambridge University Press.

Bonnstetter, R. J. (1998). Inquiry: Learning from the past with an eye on the future. *Electronic Journal of Science Education*, 3(1). Retrieved February 10, 2012, from http://unr.edu/homepage/jcannon/ejse/bonnstetter.html

Boudah, D., & Knight, S. L. (1999). Creating learning communities of research and practice: Participatory research and development. In D. Byrd & J. McIntyre (Eds.), *Research on professional development schools: Teacher education yearbook VII* (pp. 97–114). Thousand Oaks, CA: Corwin.

Bransford, J., Brown, A., & Cocking, R. (Eds.). (1999). *How people learn: Brain, mind, experience, and school.* Washington, DC: National Academy Press.

Bransford, J., Brown, A., & Cocking, R. (Eds.). (2000). *How people learn: Brain, mind, experience, and school* (expanded ed.). Washington, DC: National Academy Press.

Clandinin, D. J., & Connelly, F. M. (1996). Teachers' professional knowledge landscapes: Teacher stories. Stories of teachers. School stories. Stories of schools. *Educational Researcher* 25(3), 24–30.

Cochran-Smith, M., & Donnell, K. (2006). Practioner inquiry: Blurring the boundaries of research and practice. In J. L. Green, G. Camilli, & P. B. Elmore (Eds.), *Handbook of complementary methods in education research* (pp. 503–518). Mahwah, NJ: Lawrence Erlbaum Associates.

Cochran-Smith, M., & Lytle, S. L. (1999). The teacher research movement: A decade later. *Educational Researcher* 28(7), 15–25.

Cochran-Smith, M., & Lytle, S. (2004). Practitioner inquiry, knowledge, and university culture. In J. Loughran, M. L. Hamilton, V. LaBoskey, & T. Russell (Eds.), *International handbook of research of self-study of teaching and teacher education practices* (pp. 601–650). Amsterdam, Netherlands: Kluwer Academic.

Cole, A., & Knowles, G. (2001). *Lives in context: The art of life history research.* Lanham, MD: Rowland Altamira.

Duschl, R. (2008). Science education in three-part harmony: Balancing conceptual, epistemic, and social learning goals. *Review of Research in Education* 32(1), 268–291.

Freedman, S. (2001). Teacher research and professional development: Purposeful planning or serendipity. In A. Lieberman & L. Miller (Eds.), *Teachers caught in the action: Professional development that matters* (pp. 188–208). New York: Teachers College Press.

Fuchs D., & Fuchs, L. S. (1990). Making educational research more important. *Exceptional Children, 57*(2), 102–107.

Hargreaves, A. (2003) *Teaching in the knowledge society: Education in the age of insecurity.* New York: Teachers College Press.

Hobson, M. (2009). *Teacher perceptions of change in leadership roles and activities as a result of participation in a science education leadership program.* (Unpublished doctoral dissertation, Texas A&M University, College Station).

Kagan, D. (1990). Ways of evaluating teacher cognition: Inferences concerning the Goldilocks Principle. *Review of Educational Research, 60*(3), 419–469.

Knight, S. (2003, April). *Using action research to bridge the gap between science and educational research.* Paper presented at the annual meeting of the American Educational Research Association, Chicago.

Knight, S., & Boudah, D. (2003) Participatory research and development. In D. Wiseman & S. Knight (Eds.), *The impact of school–university collaboration on K–12 student outcomes.* Washington, DC: American Association of Colleges of Teacher Education.

Knight, S., Pedersen, S., & Morales, A., (2006, April). *Critical components for producing new leadership in science education: The contribution of the Summer II education team experience to the transportable model.* Paper presented at the annual meeting of the American Educational Research Association, San Francisco.

Knight, S., Pedersen, S., Vannest, K., Stuessy, C., & Ormiston, C. (2005, April). *Examining the impact of participation in building communities of learners on teachers' perceptions and performance.* Paper presented at the annual meeting of the American Educational Research Association, Montreal, Canada.

Lehrer, R., & Schauble, L. (2004). Modeling natural variation through distribution. *American Educational Research Journal, 41*(3), 635–679.

Lesh, R. A., & Doerr, H. M. (2003). *Beyond constructivism: Models and modeling perspectives on mathematics teaching, learning, and problem solving.* Mahwah, N.J.: Lawrence Erlbaum Associates.

Little, J. (1993). Teachers' professional development in a climate of educational reform. *Educational Evaluation and Policy Analysis, 15,* 129–151.

Lytle, S. L., & Cochran-Smith, M. (1994). Inquiry, knowledge, and practice. In S. Hollingsworth & H. Sockett (Eds.), *Teacher research and educational reform: Ninety-third yearbook of the National Society for the Study of Education* (pp. 22–51). Chicago: University of Chicago Press.

Minstrell, J. (2000). Implications for teaching and learning inquiry. In J. Minstrell & E. H. van Zee (Eds.), *Inquiring into inquiry learning and teaching in science* (pp. 471–496). Washington, DC: American Association for the Advancement of Science.

Moseley, S., & Schielack, J. F. (2005, April). *Investigating the relationship between science team functionality and participants' perceptions and products.* Paper presented at the annual meeting of the American Educational Research Association, Montreal, Canada.

National Research Council (NRC). (2000). *Inquiry and the National Science Education Standards: A guide for teaching and learning.* Washington, DC: National Academy Press.

Putnam, R., & Borko, H. (2000). What do new views of knowledge and thinking have to say about research on teacher learning? *Educational Researcher, 29*(1), 4–15.

Richardson, V., & Placier, P (2001). Teacher change. In V. Richardson (Ed.), *Handbook of research on teaching* (4th ed., pp. 905–947). Washington, DC: American Educational Research Association.

Rogoff, B., & Lave, J. (1984). *Everyday cognition.* Cambridge, MA: Harvard University Press.

Rosenholtz, S. (1989). *Teachers' workplace: The social organization of schools.* New York: Longman.

Schecter, S., & Parkhurst, S. (1993). Ideological divergences in a teacher-research group. *American Educational Research Journal, 30,* 771–798.

Shulman, L. S. (1986). Those who understand: Knowledge growth in teaching. *Educational Researcher, 15*(2), 4–14.

Shulman, L. S. (2000). From Minsk to Pinsk: Why a scholarship of teaching and learning? *The Journal of Scholarship of Teaching and Learning (JoSoTL), 1*(1), 48–53.

Smylie, M. A., & Denny, J. W. (1990). Teacher leadership: Tensions and ambiguities in organizational perspective. *Educational Administration Quarterly, 26*(3), 235–259.

Vygotsky, L. (1986). *Thought and language* (A. Kozulin, Trans.). Cambridge, MA: MIT Press.

Zeichner, K., & Noffke, S. (2001). Practitioner research. In V. Richardson (Ed.), *Handbook of research on teaching* (4th ed., pp. 260–298). Washington, DC: American Educational Research Association.

CHAPTER 6

Creating Synergy Through a Shared Research Agenda

Cathleen C. Loving, Jane F. Schielack,
Stephanie L. Knight, and Carol Stuessy

In characterizing the Information Technology in Science (ITS) Learning Ecology for science education leadership, Anderson and Minstrell in Chapter 10 suggest that "diversity of the membership . . . calls for the creation of structures, knowledge, tools, and processes that both accommodate and mediate the various professional cultures of origin," allowing for the successful creation of a functional *culture apart.* In Chapters 3, 4, and 5, authors considered IT-based inquiry, an Integrated Professional Development Model (IPDM), and practitioner research as three elements needed to create the synergy necessary for the establishment of a functional culture apart. The purpose of this chapter is to discuss a fourth way to create that synergy: through the design of a shared research agenda across the various disciplines of the members involved in the ITS Learning Ecology. The shared research agenda refers to the collaborative research undertaken in the Science Learning Communities (SLCs) and, often, the publications that resulted from the work.

Why was a shared research agenda considered necessary for creating synergy in the ITS Learning Ecology? Since the overarching commitment was to transfer current science practice into classrooms, all researchers' roles and interests in the generation of new knowledge needed to, in some way, contribute to that focus. In order to promote intellectual growth across the diverse components of the ITS Learning Ecology, science educators, instructional technologists, educational psychologists, scientists in various disciplines, graduate students in both science and science education, and grade 7–16 practitioners all needed to be equal partners in the research agenda. Since each member's individual background was unique, it was important to have a common vision of where each person, both as a researcher and a possible subject, might contribute to and benefit from the research agenda.

A CONCEPTUAL FRAMEWORK FOR
A SHARED RESEARCH AGENDA

In order for members of the ITS Learning Ecology to design their collaborative research in thoughtful ways around project goals, we felt it necessary to have a conceptual framework for conducting research within a widely diverse group. In our search for examples of this type of conceptual framework, we evaluated the examples based on our desired outcome of quality research addressing a complex system that would be considered of value in a variety of settings.

There are a number of research studies on science teacher professional development projects that cover many of the variables occurring in complex or large-scale studies (see e.g., Garet, Porter, Desimone, Birman, & Yoon, 2001; Roehrig & Luft, 2006; Penuel, Fishman, Yamaguchi, & Gallagher, 2007). The authorship of publications resulting from projects like these is often limited to the principal and co-principal investigators and one or two lead directors. We wanted to push more in the direction of multiple publications that contributed to the creation of knowledge about some aspect of the transfer of science practice into classrooms while providing opportunities for everyone in the SLCs to experience authorship of a research article. The authorship of chapters in this book reflects this goal.

Several complex projects during the last 20 years have used design experiment research strategies (Brown, 1992) to enable multiyear projects to develop early proto-theories as research designs evolved. A good example of coordinating multiple levels of analysis is described in Cobb, Confrey, diSessa, Lehrer, and Schauble (2003). The research team in such a case might have to study a whole array of norms, practices, and teacher content and pedagogical content knowledge, as well as both teacher and student reasoning about instruction and about a particular science domain. And, although design experiment components (as described in Chapter 4) were certainly evident in the long-term development of the ITS Learning Ecology, they only partially addressed our goals for extended engagement in research by all participants.

Taking a Complex Systems Approach

Another way to look at shared research is from a complex systems perspective, which is also covered more in Chapter 10 (Lemke & Sabelli, 2008). Concepts such as system–environment interaction, developmental trajectories, and varieties of self-organization are becoming tools for "qualitative reasoning about complex socio-natural systems as well as for quantitative modeling and simulation" (p. 119). This approach requires collaboration among a diverse community of researchers. As Lemke and Sabelli acknowledge, questions matter. "[Questions] are the seeds from which new theories grow, and like all seeds they carry forward the prior theories from which they come" (p. 120). Complex systems research acknowledges time scales sometimes on the order of decades and explains why change can take so long and be so difficult. And yet, ultimately, change is local. Complex systems are, in some special sense, treated as *individuals*, whether or not they are also members of some species. Our information technology-based learning ecology was certainly a complex system, so we began to delve deeper into the theory of research within a complex system. The need to find a conceptual framework that worked for the ITS Learning Ecology's shared research agenda led to the discovery of a number of similarities with another *messy* environment—an informal learning environment—a museum.

Schauble, Leinhardt, and Martin (1997) succeeded in organizing a cumulative research agenda for a museum environment that also seemed to address the needs of the information technology-based learning ecology. While the ITS Learning Ecology was in many ways very different from a museum environment, the two shared certain features. First and foremost, both environments consisted of components and characteristics that could be well explained through the use of sociocultural theory. The emphasis in the ITS Learning Ecology, as in the museum environment (Schauble et al., 1997), was on the interplay between individuals acting in social contexts (the SLCs) and the mediators with which the individuals interacted (e.g., the various information technology tools, the Student Inquiry Framework, and the Practitioner Research Plan). In our study of the ITS Learning Ecology, as in the other group's research with their museum, we were "interested not only in understanding learning but also in engineering productive forms of it" (Schauble et al., 1997, p. 4), an interest that was very much related to our design experiment approach. In general, the ITS Learning Ecology and the informal science environment shared three main features: variability across many components, an interest in the processes of learning, and the need for a developmental approach to the study of the learning in the environment. Based on these characteristics related to sociocultural theory, Schauble and colleagues focused on three major integrating research themes: (1) learning and learning environments; (2) interpretation, meaning, and explanation; and (3) identity, motivation, and interest. By analyzing and adapting Schauble and colleagues' three themes for informal learning environments and integrating our understanding of these within the design experiment framework we had adopted, we were able to build a conceptual framework within which to situate our unique shared research agenda.

Designing Experiences

The first theme presented by Schauble and colleagues (1997) is that in complex environments such as the ITS Learning Ecology, the design of the learning environment is tied closely to how learning occurs. In relation to this theme, we developed a group of research questions focusing on what type of learning environment would be best for the practitioners and for the graduate students. (See "Questions Asked" in the section "Characteristics of the Shared Research Agenda.") In addition, we wanted to investigate what kind of learning environment would result in science and education faculty working in tandem in the various settings of the synergistic inquiry experience. These questions, and some of the resulting research, demanded teams of researchers diverse in their expertise, experience, and disciplines. As in a design experiment model, much time was spent designing and redesigning learning environments based on the data collected and analyzed over time (see Chapter 4).

Clarifying Components

The second theme that prevailed among the varied group of participants within this complex project involved the interpretation, meaning, and explanation resulting from the participants' shared experiences (Schauble et al., 1997). Since our entire project was based on having participants experience science inquiry using information technology, a significant amount of time was spent asking questions about how the word *inquiry* is interpreted by different scientists and how the so-called scientific method is really portrayed and explained in their world, as compared to other explanations (see Duschl & Grandy, 2008).

The term *information technology* (IT) was, from the first days of the project's conception, deemed the big unifier among an array of scientists and engineers initially interested in the project. But neither the science educators nor the practitioners were ready for the huge array of differing meanings attached to those two words when they were applied to certain projects. The computer simulations, thousands of existing data sets, online scientific modeling, and gathering and analyzing data with probes and other sophisticated peripheral computer equipment were new to many participants (see Chapter 3). Early discussions had to specify that simply using a software program to do a slide presentation or lecture did not constitute using IT. Thus a number of shared research questions had to do with clarifying interpretations, meanings, and explanations of important components of the ITS Learning Ecology.

Exploring Engagement

Finally, Schauble and colleagues (1997) found it helpful to characterize a third theme of research in the unique setting of a museum, but applicable to other complex learning environments as well, involving identity, motivation, and interest. So, too, in our learning ecology, various individual trajectories led some faculty and graduate students into involvement for as long as 6 years.

Research interests grew out of this extended participation that were concerned with how participants saw themselves as learners, the motivation driving their initial interest, and what sustained their interest once they were involved in the learning ecology (see also Chapters 7, 8, and 9).

CHARACTERISTICS OF THE SHARED RESEARCH AGENDA

The themes evident in museum environments led to discussions about their implications for research within the ITS Learning Ecology. The rationale for and complexity of the shared research agenda required us to consider the question: "How is doing research in this synergistic learning ecology different from research done in a single principal investigator project in terms of *questions asked, methodologies used,* and *attributions made?*" The analysis of this question led to the identification of characteristics in these areas that were specific to our shared research agenda.

Questions Asked

As the ITS Learning Ecology evolved, active participants consistently expressed interest in important research questions that continued to remain largely unanswered in the literature on improving science teaching and learning. These questions tended to be multifaceted, with their investigation requiring the distributed expertise that existed in our diverse group of faculty, graduate students, and practitioners. The nature of this complex, multitiered project required that for questions posed to be meaningful, they often had to be very comprehensive. These complex questions then had to be deconstructed into sets of questions that addressed researchable components related to each of the themes in the theoretical research framework. For example, consider the following complex question: "What does it take to translate a scientist's inquiry into inquiry that practitioners can successfully implement in classrooms?" If we deconstruct this question into researchable components, it becomes a series of related questions within the three research themes.

Research questions targeting the design of experiences focused heavily on the interaction between the participants and the learning environment, including the following:

- What background science knowledge do practitioners need to have to be comfortable with the inquiry, allowing them to take some form of it to their classroom?

- How best can that knowledge be assessed and monitored by both scientists and practitioners themselves, since practitioners come from different science disciplines?
- What technological knowledge and skills do practitioners need?
- What pedagogical content knowledge do practitioners need?
- What educational knowledge do scientists need in order to effectively plan their 3-week inquiry sessions?
- What knowledge do practitioners need in order to grow as researchers in their own classrooms?

Research questions that targeted clarification of components of the ITS Learning Ecology were designed to uncover the similarities and differences among the diverse members, for example:

- How and why do various scientists do the inquiry they do? What common features and what unique features make scientists' work differ from the work of one another (cognitive, social, epistemological)?
- What is the best way for science educators and scientists to move toward communicating with a shared language when it initially seems apparent that this is not the case?
- How much time does it take for a diverse team of researchers to interpret, analyze, and synthesize results effectively when we know each member has a unique lens—and there are decidedly social aspects to each participant's contribution, from the professor–student relationship to the scientist–science educator relationship to the new relationships formed between two or more scientists from different disciplines? (In some ways we provided an excellent participant pool for a study of the sociological aspects of knowledge construction.)

A third set of research questions focused on initial engagement and sustainability. These questions included the following:

- What logistical support do practitioners need in schools to implement inquiry successfully?
- What rewards, challenges, or barriers exist when inquiry is attempted in classrooms?
- What rewards, challenges, or barriers exist when research related to inquiry is undertaken by practitioners in the classroom?
- What are effective ways to increase the sense of ownership and the collaborative role in the project's research plan for all researchers?

Methodologies

One of the advantages of being involved in shared research is that we learned much about different methodologies from new colleagues. For example, scientists improved significantly in understanding how people learn and how to apply this knowledge to assess learning in their specific content areas. Education researchers and practitioners became familiar with new fields of science and engineering and learned from science faculty and graduate students more about the IT-based methodologies used in those fields to gather data. Doctoral students in science education taught science graduate students about several qualitative methods, such as case study and semistructured interview protocols. Some of the exchanges between experts in different fields were challenging as we all navigated through one another's varied knowledge and backgrounds.

Out of this messy array of research tools and methodologies came what might be called engaged learning curves. A variety of methodologies were introduced and applied on an as-needed basis, and no one was pressured beyond his or her interests or capabilities. Virtually all participants were learning about methodologies in new fields as they were trying to address research questions that were different from the usual array in their own fields. In some instances, comparisons were made in research methodologies across fields in order to clarify situations and stimulate thinking. For example, a geologist and an educational researcher found several similarities between field research in geology and educational research in the classroom. Both require uncovering the information of importance within a complex, constantly changing setting; both involve a plethora of uncontrollable extraneous variables; and both involve taking a snapshot of the present and situating it in a meaningful history.

Many of the research questions explored in the different SLCs were of the type that were best answered by assessing whether grade 7–16 students performed inquiry better as a result of the practitioners' participation in the ITS Learning Ecology. However, separate sets of data drawn from the investigations of these individual research questions about student learning did not necessarily mean that we had the data to adequately address the overarching question. A unique attribute of shared research is the necessity to aggregate separate sets of data into some type of meta-data that allows the formation of explanations that reach across individual data sets. All members of the ITS Learning Ecology were required to provide input for and critique of the design of the methodologies for this type of analysis, as this type of research was new to everyone. It became clear to all involved that there was an important tension involved between the large amount of time and energy required for working within a shared research agenda and the professional benefits accrued. To ensure that engagement in work with the meta-data was beneficial to all members, discussions of ideas about methodologies for this highest level of research became the focus of monthly research meetings and the topic of several retreats.

Opportunities for Involvement

Members of the ITS Learning Ecology agreed that it was important that a shared research agenda provide opportunities for all who wanted to be involved in the many areas of research related to inquiry and the use of information technology. Research interests were regularly listed on the research link of the ITS Learning Ecology's website. Although many research groups formed from the membership of an SLC, some research interests cut across several SLCs, for example, an investigation of the use of concept mapping. All members of the learning ecology were encouraged to add interests or join a group that wanted to do a particular research project. The site for proposing a research project asked for a title, lead contact, description, dissemination plans, research questions, possible collaborators, data sources, and target dates. Typically, the lead contact would remain first author and the group would meet to decide the work distribution and order of authors. When examined after 6 years, this list had 22 graduate student entries and 11 faculty/staff entries for research projects (with a few repeats). The number of collaborators ranged from one to nine for each project.

PRODUCTS OF THE SHARED RESEARCH AGENDA

While everyone started out "rooted in their home department," as Anderson and Minstrell suggest in Chapter 10, faculty and graduate students began to stretch their interests into new fields. Scientists and their graduate students began conducting educational research. Science education researchers began studies with scientists about how the scientists did their work (Loving, Sulikowski, Anderson, & Minstrell, 2005). The mix of education and graduate students—and the ascension of some from the role of participant to Campus Resource Person (CRP), in which they mentored other participants—afforded an opportunity for all to begin to ask research questions in new areas of interest.

Following are examples of some of the research published from the shared research agenda in the ITS Learning Ecology. The three previously described themes of designing experiences, clarifying components, and exploring engagement appear across three major areas of interest.

Research on the Impact of Information Technology in Grade 7–16 Science Education

Since all interdisciplinary SLCs used information technology as an integral part of their 3-week sessions, a main goal of the synergistic inquiry experience was to introduce grade 7–12 practitioners to the use of IT for inquiry in their classrooms. Some of the Practitioner Research Plans (PRPs) are described in Chapter 5. In particular, two practitioners who became science education graduate students designed research projects that resulted in theses. Scallon (2006), a former middle school science teacher who became an assistant professor in education, started her research as a result of her experiences in the Plant Genomics Learning Community. She started her work with a biologist and science educator who introduced her to inexpensive equipment to take time-lapse photographs to monitor plant growth and movement. Bryan (2006), a doctoral student who became an assistant professor in physics education, became interested in his dissertation topic of using simulations to teach physics concepts as a result of his participation in a synergistic inquiry experience involving software that supported taking measurements from videotaped phenomena.

Research on the Impact of Information Technology in Undergraduate Education

There were numerous opportunities for science and education professors, along with graduate students teaching undergraduates, to engage in research involving technologies used in the SLCs. Several examples highlight the array of interdisciplinary collaboration, an important attribute of the shared research agenda. Sell, Herbert, Stuessy, and Schielack (2006) investigated the use of information technology to provide multiple representations to support inquiry in a geology course. In this study a geology student, a geology professor, a science educator, and a mathematics educator worked together to craft questions and methodologies. In Ezrailson, Allen, and Loving (2004), a science education doctoral student (who became an assistant professor of science education), a mathematics professor, and a science educator explored the impact of a specific technology application on a specific physics concept. Simmons, Wu, Knight, and Lopez (2008) reflected the collaboration of a landscape ecologist, an educational psychology professor, and two graduate students in the implementation of a Geographic Information Systems-based inquiry component in ecology classes and the impact of these components on student learning and motivation.

Research on the Impact of the ITS Learning Ecology on Participants

A third area of shared research was centered around how participation impacted the members of the ITS Learning Ecology. The following examples illustrate the variety of perspectives that were addressed in this category of research. Ford, Bevan, Besok, and Schielack (2005) combined their perspectives from chemical engineering, mechanical engineering, and mathematics education to analyze the participation of the members of the Nanotechnology Learning Community.

Ruebush and colleagues (2009) summarized the experiences of the members of the Molecular View of the Environment Learning Community, including analyses of the engagement of both the lead scientists and the practitioners.

A more in-depth analysis of faculty participants appears in Loving and colleagues (2005). In this research, a science educator, a master's student in science education who already had a PhD in chemistry, and two external evaluators examined scientists' understanding of the grade 7–12 environment and the extent to which they changed their attitudes and beliefs about grade 7–12 science education as they participated in the ITS Learning Ecology. Two case studies (Loving & Herbert, 2006) were conducted to further investigate impacts on faculty, revealing unique trajectories for each of the two scientists and different reasons for becoming involved. Both scientists revealed in interviews that they were reassured by the commitment of science educators and practitioners. Each went on to revise or design new undergraduate courses with more emphasis on inquiry. Both have since won teaching awards, and both are involved in large funded projects involving science education and inquiry.

BENEFITS OF A SHARED RESEARCH AGENDA

In an appearance before the House Commerce, Justice, and Science Subcommittee in 2010, Professor Julie Luft (2010) of Arizona State University made a case for the support of science education. In particular, she asked for support of a science-as-inquiry approach that required scientists and educators to work together, each having vital roles in the presentation, translation, and preparation of new science teachers. She also suggested the need for supporting long-term research studies, as is already done in science and medicine. Going beyond a few years, she stated, the long-term research could improve what we know in science education and how best learning can occur. Finally, Luft called for better translation of research into practice, with the suggestion that "placing research in the hands of teachers is critical if we are going to change how science teachers teach."

After 6 years of effort, our ITS Learning Ecology became an environment that could address the call for long-term research, produced by teams of scientists and educators, that eventually transforms practice. In addition, the shared research agenda helped reinvigorate the academic pool of future professors of science and science education. Scores of new students were involved in graduate programs, with many of the ITS Learning Ecology faculty in both science and education taking lead roles in initial advising and committee membership.

These accomplishments were not without challenges, however. The messiness mentioned at the beginning of this chapter lingered in many areas. Scientists who joined the project were not walking into something that had a step-by-step process—when sometimes their own science had become at least predictable in its margin of error. This was a large hurdle for some. They had to believe both that they wanted to help practitioners and that the people they were trying to help were worthy. In fact, each group of participants had learning curves related to how to interact effectively with others. The shared research experiences stood out as one of the most successful ways to find common interests and to reach common understandings.

Of particular note are the graduate students who participated in these shared research experiences and have gone on to positions in higher education. In every case, the nature of their interdisciplinary work, their being free to take the lead, and their increased comfort level with the work in other fields actually made them stand out in an otherwise slow job market. While research (Rheten & Parker, 2004) suggests that there are both risks and rewards of an interdisciplinary research path, our graduate students without exception seem to have benefited.

REFERENCES

Brown, A. L. (1992). Design experiments: Theoretical and methodological challenges in creating complex interventions in classroom settings. *Journal of the Learning Sciences, 2*(2), 141–178.

Bryan, J. (2006). Technology for physics instruction. *Contemporary Issues in Technology and Teacher Education* [Online serial], *6*(2). Retrieved February 10, 2012, from http://www.citejournal.org/vol6/iss2/science/article2.cfm

Cobb, P., Confrey, J., diSessa, A., Lehrer, R., & Schauble, L. (2003). Design experiments in educational research. *Educational Researcher, 32*(1), 9–13.

Duschl, R., & Grandy, R. (Eds.). (2008). *Teaching scientific inquiry: Recommendations for research and implementation.* Rotterdam, Netherlands: Sense Publishers.

Ezrailson, C. M., Allen, G. D., & Loving, C. C. (2004). Analyzing pendulum motion in an interactive online environment using Flash. *Science and Education 13*(4–5), 437–457.

Ford, D. M., Bevan, M. A., Besok, A., & Schielack, J. (2005, November). *High school science teachers use scientific inquiry in nanotechnology.* Paper presented at the annual meeting of the American Institute of Chemical Engineers, Cincinnati, OH.

Garet, M. S., Porter, A. C., Desimone, L., Birman, B. F., & Yoon, K. S. (2001). What makes professional development effective? Results from a national sample of teachers. *American Educational Research Journal 38*(4), 915–945.

Lemke, J., & Sabelli, N. (2008). Complex systems and educational change: Towards a new research agenda. *Educational Philosophy and Theory, 40*(1).

Loving, C. C., & Herbert, B. E. (2006, April). *Portraits of a diverse group of scientists in the ITS project.* Paper presented at the annual meeting of the American Educational Research Association, San Francisco, CA.

Loving, C. C., Sulikowski, M., Anderson, R., & Minstrell, J. (2005, April) *Examining the impact of participation in building communities of learners: Science faculty attitudes and practices.* Paper presented at the annual meeting of the American Educational Research Association, Montreal, Canada.

Luft, J. (2010, February 4). Presentation to House Commerce, Justice, and Science Subcommittee. Retrieved August 25, 2011, from http://democrats.appropriations.house.gov/images/stories/pdf/cjs/2011_STEM_Ed_Hearing_2_Luft_testimony.pdf

Penuel, W. R., Fishman, B. J., Yamaguchi, R., & Gallagher, L. P. (2007). What makes professional development effective? Strategies that foster curriculum implementation. *American Educational Research Journal, 44*(4), 921–958.

Rheten, D., & Parker, A. (2004). Risks and rewards of an interdisciplinary research path. *Science, 306,* 2046.

Roehrig, G. H., & Luft, J. A. (2006). Does one size fit all? The induction experience of beginning science teachers from different teacher-preparation programs. *Journal of Research in Science Teaching, 43*(9), 963–985.

Ruebush, L. E., Grossman, E. L., Miller, S. A., North, S. W., Schielack, J. F., & Simanek, E. E. (2009). Scientists' perspective on introducing authentic inquiry to high school teachers during an intensive three-week summer professional development experience. *School Science and Mathematics Journal 109*(3), 162–174.

Scallon, J. M. (2006). *Comparative study of authentic scientific research versus guided inquiry in affecting middle school students' abilities to know and do genetics.* Unpublished master's thesis, Texas A&M University, College Station.

Schauble, L., Leinhardt, G., & Martin, L. (1997). A framework for organizing a cumulative research agenda in informal learning contexts. *Journal of Museum Education, 22*(2&3), 3–8.

Sell, K. S., Herbert, B. E., Stuessy, C., & Schielack, J. (2006). Supporting student conceptual model development of complex earth systems through the use of multiple representations and inquiry, *Journal of Geoscience Education, 54,* 396–407.

Simmons, M., Wu, X. B., Knight, S., & Lopez, R. (2008). Assessing the influence of field- and GIS-based inquiry on student attitude and conceptual knowledge in an undergraduate ecology laboratory. *Cell Biology Education—Life Sciences Education, 7,* 338–345.

Part III

PERSPECTIVES OF THE IT-BASED LEARNING ECOLOGY EXPERIENCE: IMPACTS

"We see beautiful adaptation everywhere" (from C. R. Darwin in *On the origin of species by means of natural selection, or the preservation of favoured races in the struggle for life*, published by John Murray, London, 1859, p. 61).

These three chapters present analyses of the ITS Learning Ecology from different viewpoints: from the system perspective, from the community perspective, and from the perspectives of various populations. Chapter 7 presents a model of the working structure of the ITS Learning Ecology, highlighting the assessment of the degree and quality of connectivity in the system. Chapter 8 discusses the successful characteristics and strategies that emerged from the heterogeneous learning communities and explores the broader implications regarding connections between current science and classrooms. Chapter 9 examines the interactions and patterns of adaptation for each of the three principal populations in the learning ecology: university faculty, graduate students, and practitioners.

CHAPTER 7

Connectivity in the IT-Based Learning Ecology: A System Perspective

George M. Nickles and Bruce Herbert

The term *ecology* indicates a complex web of interactions among diverse parts of a system (X. B. Wu, personal communication, April 2008). As discussed in previous chapters, the Information Technology in Science (ITS) Learning Ecology was made up of people from diverse fields of study and experience. Having people with this level of diversity interact and develop into an effective network that supports the ecology of the program required time and concerted effort. An ecological system does not spring into existence instantaneously. Nor does a program of this nature instantaneously develop a leadership team that collaborates effectively around a shared set of goals. This chapter focuses on the ITS program management team—specifically, how the team developed the necessary shared knowledge, goals, and language to lead an interdisciplinary system.

The management team was the main means through which the personnel in the science education leadership program interacted. The team oversaw the program's activities and was a central driver for the ITS Learning Ecology. The role of the team evolved and changed over time as the program progressed and matured and as leadership roles were taken at more local levels in the system. The growth and development of the team is described here and shown to have been an integral structure for the effective functioning of this learning ecology.

MANAGEMENT TEAM MEMBERSHIP AND ACTIVITIES

While a program may have a director to oversee day-to-day operations, a management team is typically responsible for setting the overall goals and plans and evaluating progress toward those goals. It was recognized from the beginning of the project that the management team needed to include the major stakeholders even if (and especially if) they were situated across very different disciplines. (See Chapter 1 for more detail on the makeup of the management team.)

By the third cohort of the project (with each cohort a 2-year round of Science Learning Communities), the management team typically met once a month during the academic year to discuss the synergistic inquiry experience and ways to improve it. Meetings were relatively informal and typically had a collaborative spirit whereby the members came together to discuss general and specific issues from their diverse perspectives. The management team existed continually from the beginning of the program, changing focus and membership as needed but remaining a central group within the ITS Learning Ecology.

EVOLUTION OF THE MANAGEMENT TEAM

We address the evolution of the management team and how effectively it functioned in three ways. First, we examine the discussions of the team over time to determine if there was a change in their focus that corresponded to changing membership of the team and key points in the ITS Center's development. Second, we examine the adaptability of the team to feedback from external evaluation. Third, we look at the management team in the midst of the final cohort to determine to what degree team members had a shared conception of the goals of the program.

Change in Focus

We would expect to see a change in the content of the discussions of the team over time as the ITS Learning Ecology grew and matured, the synergistic learning experience went through major revisions through three cohorts, and the members of the team learned to work together. The discussions would be expected to reflect the shift from building a program from scratch to implementing improvements. These improvements included moving from topics such as examining goals, to developing a shared understanding and set of terms and educational theory, to more practical decision making for the project and its evaluation.

To examine how the management team's discussions changed over time, we took the minutes recorded at each meeting between August 2000 and June 2003 and categorized their contents. The management team met less frequently after the 2002–2003 academic year, so comparisons with discussions after this time is problematic. We hypothesized that all the discussion points in the minutes could be categorized into five main topics: philosophy of the ITS Learning Ecology (e.g., discussions of theories that should guide the work, coming to a consensus on definitions of terms), research efforts (e.g., current research and dissemination within and about the program), design of the synergistic inquiry experience, implementation of evaluation and assessment, and pragmatic issues (e.g., scheduling meetings). This analysis served as a starting point for our categorization efforts.

Figure 7.1 shows the percentage of the total discussion items dedicated to each category for each semester. While there are fluctuations across semesters for the categories, one clear trend is the decrease over time in the percentage of discussion items related to the philosophy and design of the ITS Learning Ecology. This decrease reaches the point that such discussions are nearly nonexistent in the 2002–2003 academic year. This trend is indicative of the management team's moving past the phase of developing a shared philosophy and structure to more collaboration on particulars of the implementation of the project. (This is consistent with the evolution of the design process described in Chapter 4.)

Adaptations Based on Feedback

Another aspect of the management team that was examined was its responsiveness to feedback. Our external evaluators were responsible for providing formative evaluation data on the program to guide improvements and examine

Figure 7.1. Management Team Discussion Topics

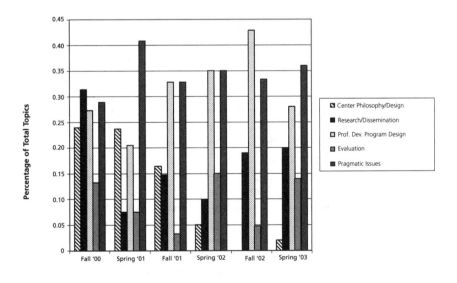

the work of the management team. While evaluation of the management team was not uniformly positive through all its aspects over all years, the following quotes—in which "the Center" refers to the ITS Learning Ecology—show that the team grew and proved to be adaptive.

In the first year's report, the evaluators wrote:

> In most cases the Center staff was responsive to suggestions for situations that could be improved in the short term. . . . The Center staff is aware of these concerns and others. They have been responsive and committed to addressing concerns during their activities for this year and in planning for next summer.

An excerpt from the third year's report notes:

> Communication is another area in which the Center staff has made particularly good progress. While this has been an ITS forte from the onset, there have also been some key improvements that attest to the Center staff's responsive nature and dedication to ongoing refinement and improvement of the program.

In the fourth year's report, the leadership is described as "supportive but adaptive." And it is noted that "[c]entralized, supportive, responsive and efficient describe the ITS Center's organization."

Development of Shared Understandings

The management team faced several barriers in the discussions of the ITS Learning Ecology's philosophy and design and the progression toward adaptability. These barriers can be categorized in three ways: language/communication barriers, discipline barriers, and ownership barriers. It is difficult to discuss these separately because they are intertwined in the ecology. No one issue necessarily was addressed *first* so much as they all had to be overcome together.

The language and discipline barriers are closely related, yet distinct. Those in the field of education use specific terminology that is not widely known in other fields. Indeed, specialized terminology exists for nearly any discipline (or specialty in a discipline), yet the problem is exacerbated by the nature of the discipline. Since the educational enterprise is pervasive throughout our society, there is an assumption that education is a commonly understood field. Also, since nearly all university faculty teach courses, there is the assumption that any faculty member understands the field of education (Adams, 2002; Gaff, 2002). In reality, teaching in a classroom is a complex task requiring knowledge and skills that are not necessarily a part of the formal education of all faculty.

This assumption is related to a discipline issue, which is that research in a scientific discipline is more valued than research on the teaching of one's discipline (Savkar & Lokere, 2010). This attitude is changing, but it remains an issue at many institutions. Also present is the frequent attitude that education is a *lesser* discipline because it does not share the level of rigorous, statistically based, strongly controlled research that exists in many scientific fields. Also, in the science disciplines, there is a tendency to approach any problem with a *divide-and-conquer* strategy. When the scientists are viewed as the content experts and education specialists as the experts in their field, then the attitude may be that one faculty member should do the work of the project that resides in that person's discipline while the work in other disciplines should be done by those experts. If the project is to be an ecological whole in which members interact symbiotically, each member must interact with other members, not attempt to work without communicating with them.

Ownership of a project can also be an issue and is intertwined with discipline. Institutions of higher education group faculty into hierarchical organizations by discipline, which is often a natural and fruitful grouping. Therefore, working across organizational boundaries (beyond simply discipline boundaries) can be problematic (Adams, 2002; Gaff, 2002). The issues may include which organizational unit *owns* the program in the sense of overseeing its operations and providing resources. Once ownership is established, personnel from outside that larger organizational unit may face barriers working across that boundary because they may feel the need to support their own organization. Also, the institution may place less value on work outside the discipline or organizational unit in terms of promotion and tenure.

Again, these barriers were not overcome easily or singly. While various formal methods were attempted to bridge the gap between scientists and educators (e.g., compiling a glossary of educational terms and providing peer-reviewed articles), a significant factor in the ITS Learning Ecology experience was simply interacting with one another in formal meetings and informal settings. A turning point for some of the scientists was seeing that education researchers also use the empirical scientific method but that the subject of their study is very different. Each student is unique, has a unique background and set of experiences, has a distinct personality and learning style, and deserves to be treated as a human being rather than a laboratory sample. The same is true for practitioners. Experimentation in this setting presents barriers not applicable to most researchers in the hard sciences.

Another element that aided this process was the shared goal of improving science education for grade 7–16 students. Scientists, education researchers, and practitioners recognized that this was a significant issue and wanted to address it. Having this shared, overarching goal provided motivation to overcome the barriers and collaborate toward that end. Also, each group recognized that the others had expertise to bring to this endeavor, leading to the goal that the management should be a symbiotic relationship, not simply one-directional.

When asked, members in each group described the process as difficult. However, after spending time in formal and informal discussions, working together on the project toward a shared goal, the management team grew together as a cohesive group.

CENTEREDNESS OF THE MANAGEMENT TEAM

The previous analyses show that the management team grew into a focused, adaptive group. We now turn to examining what the team was like once it had achieved a state of *centeredness*. While centeredness generally refers to the state of being focused on some object, centeredness in the context of groups is defined as a state where a group of people share a common set of goals and work closely together to achieve those goals (Dodd, 1997). Centeredness can be conceived of as being on a two-dimensional graph, where how *centered* the group is depends on both (1) the degree to which members share common goals and (2) the degree to which they work together to achieve them. This state of centeredness in the management team was examined through two questions:

- How similar were the conceptions of the goals of the synergistic inquiry experience among team members?
- What was the structure of the social network formed by the members of the team?

To answer these questions, members of the management team were surveyed at a planning meeting near the beginning of the third cohort. They were asked to list the goals of the synergistic inquiry experience and to rate the frequency with which they interacted with other members of the management team. Because there were several members of the management team who were officially a part of the team but were typically not able to attend meetings, a *core group* of 11 members who attended and participated regularly were identified for analysis. We believe this subset of 11 people from the full management team accurately identifies the core group that was involved in the management team's activities. From this point forward, references to the management team refer to this core group. Seven of the 11 people in the core group attended the planning meeting and were surveyed. These data are described in relation to the two questions in the following sections.

Conceptions of the Goals of the ITS Learning Ecology

From the survey, we can examine how much the members of the management team agreed on the goals of the project. Their responses indicate the extent to which the team members had a shared vision for the learning environment they were pursuing. The survey asked team members: "What are the goal(s) of the ITS [synergistic inquiry experience]?" Through a coding process, several main goals were identified that were shared by multiple people and were generally considered goals of the program. These main goals and the number of people who included each in their response are as follows:

- Six team members: practitioners learning about information technology (IT) used in science
- Five team members: practitioners learning about inquiry methods
- Two team members: interaction of practitioners, scientists, and education specialists (or some combination of these three)
- Two team members: developing education leaders

Note again that $n = 7$ out of a possible 11 core members of the management team. The first two goals were arguably the generally recognized main goals of the project, and a strong majority of the respondents included them. Interaction between roles was a key part of the ITS Learning Ecology, though only two members considered it a goal. Possibly, some interpret this aspect of the project as a means to achieve the first two goals. Finally, two members indicated the goal of developing leadership. This was an explicit goal established at the beginning of the program, though it was eclipsed over time. Yet this goal remained to some extent for some members of the management team.

These results indicate that the group was largely in agreement on the main goals and vision of the ITS Learning Ecology. Also, some goals that might have been less emphasized later compared to earlier in the life of the ITS Learning Ecology were still important.

Structure of the Social Network

We examined the social network of the management team to find the extent to which the members perceived themselves to be connected to one another. The connectedness of the group (as revealed by a social network analysis) can affect many aspects of the functioning of the team, including individuals' satisfaction with group membership and the flow of information through the group (Friedkin, 2004). Based on the data from the survey, a network of interactions was constructed. To construct the network, if a person rated his or her relationship with another with a frequency of three interactions or more, then the relationship was considered to *exist* for this analysis. Also, relationships were treated bidirectionally; that is, if at least one person in a pair considered the relationship to exist, then it existed for both persons in the pair. Although four of the team members did not complete the survey, they were included in this analysis based on responses from the other members.

We visualized the network graphically using the network visualization tool NetDraw in the software program UCINET (Borgatti, Everett, & Freeman, 2002), as seen in Figure 7.2. From this figure, we can see that one member had links to all other members while one member had only two links.

Various measures of the social network can be calculated by UCINET (Borgatti et al., 2002). These give us a sense of how connected people were in this network, implying how much they influenced one another and how easily information was able to flow through the network. The measures and their calculated values for the management team can be found in Table 7.1.

Overall, the network of people in the management team was well connected and decentralized. There was no one single, totally controlling individual on the team. While some members were more connected than others, every person would remain connected through some path even if one person was removed from the network. This supports an ecology's need for redundancy, as discussed in Chapter 10. Related to this observation, the low betweenness-centrality value indicates very little *straddling* between otherwise unconnected groups. This measure implies that there were no clique-like groups within the team that were barely connected to the larger group. Also, the network was fairly well connected. Density and degree centrality (which is the same as density when normalized) indicate that over half of the possible connections between individuals existed in the network. While this result may not seem high, it means that, on average, each individual was connected to 5.6 out of 11 other people in the group. Also supporting this conclusion, the moderately high closeness centrality indicates that there were many shortest paths between individuals, implying that the network was highly connected.

Figure 7.2. Network Formed by the Management Team (from NetDraw)

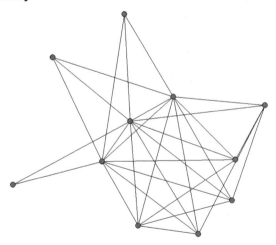

Table 7.1. Network Measures of the Management Team

Measure	Description	Meaning of Values	Value for Management Team Network
Density	Ratio of actual links between people to all possible links	0%—no links exist between people 100%—all possible links between people exist	56.36%
Betweenness Centrality	The average extent to which an individual "straddles" the communication paths of nonadjacent individuals	(normalized) Low (approaching 0)—low numbers of individuals that straddle groups (a more connected group) High (approaching 100)—high numbers of individuals that straddle groups (a less connected group)	4.848
Closeness Centrality	The average sum of the shortest distances from an individual to all other individuals in the network	(normalized) Low (approaching 0)—few individuals are on the only shortest path to other individuals (fewer individuals are central to the network) High (approaching 100)—many individuals are on the only shortest path to other individuals (more individuals are central to the network)	72.101
Degree Centrality	The average number of connections individuals have with other individuals	(normalized) Low (approaching 0)—few connections exist between individuals High (approaching 100)—individuals are highly connected to all other individuals (identical to density when normalized)	56.364

Heterogeneity

When examining the participants in the social network, we can determine the number of different disciplines represented to give a sense of the group's heterogeneity. The heterogeneity of the group can be examined by the diversity of disciplines represented on the team: one each from biology, chemistry, geoscience, industrial engineering, and mathematics education; two from educational psychology; and three from educational curriculum and instruction. In addition, one member was an administrative assistant.

The strong connections among the team members are remarkable when viewed in light of the variety of disciplines represented on the management team. In our experience, disciplines develop their own paradigm and terminology, making it difficult to communicate even similar concepts between individuals steeped in different disciplines. Taking the strength of connections and heterogeneity together, the data show that the management team overcame the discipline boundaries to focus on the goals and work of the ITS Learning Ecology. The decentralized nature of the network suggests that having no one single group or discipline in a strong leadership role allowed the diverse disciplines to work together without having a single discipline's paradigm imposed on others. This arrangement helps to address the tension of an adaptive ecology having to be both creative and stable at the same time, as discussed in Chapter 10.

LESSONS LEARNED

Some common lessons can be learned from examining the management team in the specific instance of the ITS Learning Ecology. First, the team developed and improved over time from a stance of "conscious effort" to one of "evaluate and revise." The management team went through changes as the Center progressed through cohorts. Members joined or left the group, and a shared basis of communication developed as feedback on the group's functioning was received and acted upon.

Second, the management team succeeded in forming and growing with a diverse group of people. The management team, while diverse, moved toward centeredness by developing into a decentralized, well-connected network with a generally agreed-upon set of goals. While building such teams takes time and effort, the benefits can be great. These data show that it is possible not only for such a group to form to accomplish the task but also for each member to grow and change from the experience of being part of the team.

REFERENCES

Adams, K. A. (2002). *What colleges and universities want in new faculty.* Washington, DC: Association of American Colleges and Universities.

Borgatti, S. P., Everett, M. G., & Freeman, L. C. (2002). *UCINET for Windows: Software for Social Network Analysis.* Harvard, MA: Analytic Technologies.

Dodd, C. H. (1997). *Dynamics of intercultural communication* (5th ed.). New York: McGraw-Hill.

Friedkin, N. E. (2004). Social cohesion. *Annual Review of Sociology, 30,* 409–425.

Gaff, J. G. (2002, November/December). Preparing future faculty and doctoral education. *Educational Researcher,* pp. 63–66.

Savkar, V., & Lokere, J. (2010). *Time to decide: The ambivalence of the world of science toward education.* Cambridge, MA: Nature Education.

CHAPTER 8

Bridging Current Science and Classrooms: The Science Learning Community Perspective

X. Ben Wu, Lawrence Griffing, Bruce Herbert,
Gillian Acheson, and Stephanie L. Knight

The overall function of Science Learning Communities (SLCs) in the Information Technology in Science (ITS) Learning Ecology was to support the transfer of current science and information technology to the classrooms of the practitioners. This chapter discusses the successful characteristics and strategies that emerged from the synergistic inquiry experiences in the SLCs.

Initially, the scientists in SLCs did what they are accustomed to doing in their own university classes—introduce the current science and inquiry approaches to practitioners and expect them to incorporate the current science into their instruction with the help of the education faculty. This transfer, however, required a more focused and collaborative approach to effectively bridge the current science and the classroom context in ways that change practice. Science faculty realized that they needed to work with practitioners more like they do when mentoring their graduate students than when teaching a class. Furthermore, the science faculty came to understand that mentoring was not about helping the practitioners become good scientists, as was the goal for their graduate students. Instead the purpose was to enable the practitioners to inspire the grade 7–16 students in their own classes to become scientists and informed citizens by understanding current science and scientific inquiry.

In order to focus on understanding current science and science inquiry, the scientists helped each practitioner develop an information technology (IT)-based Student Inquiry Framework (SIF) that reflected current science and fit the context of the particular classroom setting of each practitioner. These SIFs formed a key component for assessing the impact of IT-based authentic scientific inquiry on student learning. Facilitating this activity necessitated (1) understanding the prior knowledge of practitioners and the characteristics of their classrooms, (2) using effective approaches to explore current science and IT-based inquiry appropriate for classrooms of the practitioners, and (3) promoting intensive interactions among the practitioners, scientists, and education faculty.

UNDERSTANDING PRACTITIONERS' PRIOR KNOWLEDGE AND CLASSROOM SETTINGS

Understanding the characteristics of practitioners and of their classrooms was critical for developing effective SIFs. To accomplish this, a comprehensive survey of the content knowledge and experiences of the practitioners in a specific science domain was conducted by each SLC. These data were used to help design appropriate learning activities for the learning communities. The SLCs started with self-introductions by the participants about their professional training and teaching experiences as well as their classroom context. Some groups collected concept maps (Novak & Gowin, 1984) drawn by the participants to show the extent of their understanding of the interrelationships among the components of the systems to be studied. These representations not only served as tools to assess prior knowledge but also provided feedback to the scientists on the level of sophistication with which the practitioners were approaching their projects.

Discussions with practitioners about their SIFs focused on information technology tools and how existing science data sets could be used to ask interesting, relevant questions and be incorporated into doing science in the classroom. Many of the ideas generated in these discussions developed into the SIFs for the practitioners and helped the science faculty adjust subsequent learning activities to make them more relevant. Face-to-face dialogues among scientists, graduate student participants, practitioners, and education faculty further facilitated understanding about each practitioner's needs and challenges, including time constraints and standardized test expectations.

EFFECTIVE APPROACHES TO EXPLORE CURRENT SCIENCE AND AUTHENTIC INQUIRY

Several successful models emerged from the experiences of the SLCs. The following sections describe the activities and characteristics of three successful learning communities.

The Sustainable Coastal Margins Learning Community

The goal of the Sustainable Coastal Margins Learning Community was to explore the use of information technology to investigate the environmental quality of the Texas Gulf Coast from an interdisciplinary perspective. Science faculty included a biogeochemist who served as team leader, an environmental engineer, a hydrologist, and an environmental planner. The SLC also included one science education researcher; nine graduate students in geosciences, engineering, and social sciences; and two practitioners with diverse backgrounds. Scientists continually modeled the thought processes and practices that different disciplines use to study the complex nature of Earth system science.

Initially, faculty members of the SLC presented participants with a complex Earth system science environmental issue ("What is the environmental quality of the Texas Gulf Coast?") and asked them to problematize it. Faculty then modeled how they would address the issue and scaffolded the knowledge and skills needed to solve similar problems using web-based information and geospatial information technology tools. The biogeochemist led the community in collectively exploring a range of important core concepts in environmental science. The SLC visited a biogeochemistry lab, where science graduate student participants and professors discussed their research projects. Participants were introduced to ArcView GIS (geographic information system) and began learning to map using the technology.

The hydrologist led the participants in exploring the hydrology of coastal watersheds and how they are modeled. Small groups with distributed expertise estimated evaporation using data sets and modeling watersheds using GIS technology. The civil engineer had the group explore nonpoint source pollution, best management practices, and the engineering design processes. Practitioners and graduate students worked together in distributed groups using the Internet to research related topics and shared their findings with the community. They also used Excel to estimate mass loading for a year and PowerPoint to develop an animation modeling contaminant transport. They used concepts they had learned to develop a conceptual design for controlling nonpoint source pollution from a fictional watershed undergoing urbanization. Finally, the environmental planner had the group explore basic concepts in land- and resource-use patterns, socioeconomic and demographic patterns, environmental dispute resolution, and conflict management in planning. Graduate students helped practitioners use GIS to make maps showing the spatial patterns of land use and population characteristics around Corpus Christi Bay in Texas, estimate the impact on water quality, and evaluate the relationship between land use and population growth in the area. Members of the SLC proposed ways to alter land use and population patterns to both protect water quality and ensure sustainable development. As a concluding activity, practitioners presented the SIFs they had developed during the integrated professional development experience. Faculty and peers critiqued the frameworks and provided feedback for possible improvement.

Following the opportunity to implement the frameworks in their classrooms, practitioners reported their results. Again, members of the SLC critiqued the frameworks and made suggestions for overcoming any problems experienced during implementation. The group developed a digital self-guided learning module supporting scaffolding for the SIFs. The four scientists, as a group, discussed the nature of science and scientific inquiry from each of their perspectives, and the practitioners examined their frameworks to determine how they could incorporate the ideas related to the nature of science and experimental design. Some members of the community went on a field trip to the Texas Gulf Coast to see researchers at work, while others worked on spatial analysis introduced by the environmental planner. As a culminating activity for the entire community, scientists, graduate students, and practitioners worked together to explore a number of environmental case studies.

The Sustainable Coastal Margins Learning Community had three design characteristics that effectively scaffolded practitioners to transfer authentic science to the classroom through use of information technology. These characteristics included distribution of expertise within a team approach as well as use of case studies and IT-based tools.

Distributed Expertise to Explore Authentic Questions. The central question addressed by the Sustainable Coastal Margins Learning Community was engaging, poorly constrained, and allowed participants to initially approach the question from a number of perspectives that utilized their existing prior knowledge. Evaluating the environmental quality of the Texas Gulf Coast also involved a number of major concepts incorporated into the national and state science standards.

Exploration of Content Knowledge and Scientific Practices Through Case Studies. The learning community approach incorporated collaborative engagement with a range of case studies associated with environmental issues in Texas. Team leaders emphasized a cognitive apprenticeship approach that emphasized both modeling of and coaching in the authentic scientific practices that are utilized to address the community's central scientific question.

Use of Appropriate Information Technology to Produce Artifacts That Support Science Transfer to the Classroom. The Sustainable Coastal Margins Learning Community used a number of authentic IT tools, including geographic information systems and analysis of remote-sensing images, to engage in scientific studies focused on data set analysis and simulation. These tools were instrumental in supporting transfer of the science to the practitioner's classrooms by creating authentic representations and providing the means to support student engagement in scientific practices such as question generation, data analysis, and explanation development.

The Macro and Micro Imaging Learning Community

The goal of the Macro and Micro Imaging Learning Community was to bring authentic science into the classroom through IT-enabled imaging of *new* biological worlds at the micro and macro levels. The imaging was transdimensional, meaning that it crossed boundaries of time and space that are not easily observable and recorded in the classroom but are becoming more accessible through new implementation of IT-based computational technology and IT-mediated delivery of shared databases of raw information. Science faculty included a cell biologist and a plant biologist. This learning community also included one science education researcher, three graduate students in biology and six in science education, and six practitioners who taught a variety of science courses.

Plants were the organism of choice for exploring micro worlds because (1) they are cheaply exported to and grown in the classroom; (2) they have few of the constraints imposed by using, manipulating, and dissecting live animals; and (3) the scientists in the team were active plant biologists. The model plant used for participant study, *Arabidopsis thaliana*, is used by most plant molecular, genetic, and cell biologists because extensive databases of genetic sequence exist for it and because there are a wide variety of knock-outs in genes of known and unknown function. Two forms of transdimensional imaging were used: (1) time-lapse photography to reveal and record plant growth and development over a time frame not easily seen and (2) video 3D and time-lapse confocal microscopy to reveal the structure of cells on a spatial and temporal level also not typically accessible.

In the macro world, other organisms could be studied in the classroom through transdimensional imaging by means of remote cameras in distant regions. Bears and sea lions were chosen for study because (1) they are very popular animals, being wild and untamed but also fuzzy and amusing; (2) they are species that may be affected dramatically by global climate change; and (3) some of the species are on the verge of extinction, while others are endangered in several regions of the globe. Three remote cameras were used during the course of this study: one at McNeil River in Alaska to look at brown bear (grizzly) behavior and spacing along the river bank during salmon fishing, one at Chiswell Island in Alaska to look at Steller sea lions returning to breed and give birth, and one in Wolong Panda Captive Breeding Center in China to look at play behaviors of juvenile pandas in captivity.

The design characteristics that enabled this SLC to bridge current science and classroom contexts included bringing students, teachers, and scientists to the same virtual lab bench; using tools that facilitate asking good questions; and using an IT infrastructure to enable extended participation in collection and

sharing of data within the larger community of science. Each of these characteristics is described in the sections that follow.

Mechanisms to Enable All Participants to Be Science Researchers.
Transdimensional imaging through IT-enabled technology provides broader
access to the world of scientific research. The IT-mediated databases that enable the sharing of raw information bring the student and teacher to the same
IT-enabled lab bench as the professional science researcher in order to participate in the process of discovery. In the micro world, training in time-lapse
photography, plant growth and development, genetic and environmental roles
in phenotype expression, video microscopy, fluorescence microscopy, and
confocal microscopy provided the technological background that enabled the
practitioner to behave like a scientist engaged in research in the micro world of
cell dynamics and genetics, a level of scale that students find difficult to grasp.
Consequently, the Macro and Micro Imaging Learning Community practitioners had to learn, and then be able to teach, how to acquire and analyze the
information on which their SIFs were based.

Tools That Enable Practitioners to Ask Testable Questions. In micro-
world topics, members of this SLC started with guided inquiry in which the
scientists asked a testable question and ended with open inquiry in which the
practitioners asked the testable questions. Becoming a scientist consists of more
than using new technology; it is asking a testable question of scientific relevance
using this technological window on the new world. The guided inquiry provided
instruction on implementing image analysis, using free and open-source software. Practitioners (during the synergistic inquiry experience), scientists (during
their research), and students (in the classroom) obtained the data sets. The quan-
tification provided by image analysis of growing dynamic plant cells and tissues
provided a gateway to implementation of the SIFs. When moving from guided
to open inquiry, practitioners used analogies as a springboard to ask questions.
The use of analogies dovetails with existing pedagogical practice in grades 7–16,
and it was particularly fortunate that the one analogy used for the function of the
endoplasmic reticulum—that it is a transport network for the cell like a capillary
bed is for the tissue—was considered at the start of the research to be *wrong* by
the global science community but was discovered by one of the collaborators during the course of the ITS Learning Ecology to be *right* (Runions, Brach, Kühner,
& Hawes, 2006).
    Another tool for getting teachers and students to start asking questions was
the creation of concept maps. Concept maps were particularly valuable in providing information to students and teachers about how carefully environment
has to be controlled in order to see the genetic influence on phenotype. Concept
mapping is a particularly useful tool in learning complex systems, revealing the
complexity of the system and the sophistication with which students approach

the system, while providing an image of the system for group discussion (Novak & Gowin, 1984). Concept maps provided a guide to asking interesting and relevant questions within the context of mandated content.

Use of IT-Mediated Platforms to Share Data and Provide Opportunities for Participation in the Larger Community of Science. Participation in the community of science is an important aspect of community-centered science learning. Students participating in classroom laboratory experiences have few opportunities to make scientific discoveries that contribute to the community of science, primarily because the type of discoveries they make are already known or are so parochial that scientists are not interested. Scientists leading the Macro and Micro Imaging Learning Community constructed an IT infrastructure that provided teachers and their students with a means to share data and communicate with scientists prior to the publication of the findings in scientific journals. It facilitated the communication between professional scientists and students by making the teacher the scientist who can help direct and instruct the process of scientific discovery.

However, a question arises about the nature of sharing raw data through IT-mediated platforms related to determining ownership of the data, or at least recognizing an individual's involvement in the collection of the data and, subsequently, ownership of the discovery if one is made. The field is working to establish protocols for the appropriate recognition of the involvement of individuals (students, teachers, and scientists) in providing data and in making the ultimate discoveries. Protocols will vary depending on the nature of the discovery and the venue in which it is published.

The Landscape Ecology Learning Community

The Landscape Ecology Learning Community had a very diverse group of participants including researchers in landscape ecology, practitioners teaching different subjects (biology, science, physics, chemistry, mathematics, and statistics), science graduate students, and education graduate students. The focus of this community was on helping the participants develop individual SIFs that addressed spatial questions in their own subject areas using IT-based approaches for incorporation into their grade 7–16 curricula. These authentic inquiry projects were expected to be based on the current science of landscape ecology, aligned with curricular requirements, and directly relevant to the local ecological or environmental issues. The inquiry frameworks were the practitioners' creations; science faculty acted primarily as facilitators. As a result, the inquiry projects developed were diverse. Inquiry frameworks included GIS-based assessment of the influence of urbanization on the ecology of Kendall County, Texas; landscape changes and endangered species in Isiboro Secure National Park in Bolivia; spatial relations, randomness, and point-pattern analysis in Advanced Placement

(AP) statistics; Excel-based modeling of weak acid and buffer systems for AP chemistry and environmental-quality applications; scale-dependent habitat selection of whooping cranes, predicting future distribution of cattle egret rookeries using spatial-pattern analysis; integration of scale concept at multiple levels in math curricula; and spatial patterns and mechanisms of squirrel distribution on a university campus. In order to facilitate the development of these SIFs, the Landscape Ecology Learning Community took a case study approach with a flexible structure, described in the following sections, to explore current science and provided ample technical support for practitioners.

Use of Case Studies to Explore Current Theories and Inquiry Approaches. Most of the case studies were based on published and ongoing research of a team of scientists, which helped practitioners better understand the authentic inquiry process. The case studies had a strong IT component and focused on pattern-process interactions using landscape analysis, spatial statistics, and GIS modeling approaches. Guided inquiry activities were conducted in the laboratory to address spatial questions; visualization and spatial analysis of complex data sets were done using GIS and spatial statistical software. Spreadsheet-based exercises were also used to enhance understanding about the mechanisms of the analytical approaches. The case studies incorporated a wide range of research questions and spatial methods that provided rich ideas and opportunities for practitioners to incorporate current science and IT into their classrooms.

Sufficient Technical Support for the Practitioners. It was critical for practitioners to receive ample feedback, as well as sufficient technical support, during the development of their SIFs. The development of complex spatial data sets and learning software and procedures for data manipulation and analyses associated with individual SIFs posed significant technical challenges to participants. Scientists and graduate student mentors provided support to ensure that each practitioner had a functional SIF ready for use in the classroom. For example, there was interest in database applications for SIFs that had not been anticipated; consequently, several lectures and laboratory exercises using a common database program were added to meet the needs of practitioners.

DEVELOPING RELATIONSHIPS WITHIN SYMBIOTIC LEARNING COMMUNITIES

Interactions among members of a SLC, especially between practitioners and graduate students, contributed significantly to the development of the SIFs. Not only did practitioners and graduate students bring complementary expertise that helped each other, but the interactions often stimulated creative thinking that generated novel ideas and innovative ways to implement those ideas in classrooms. In order to effectively bridge the current science done at the university and in the classroom, SLC members had regular roundtable discussions, one-on-one discussions, and joint conferences of science faculty, education faculty, and other participants on how the current science research and IT approaches could be linked to grade 7–16 science classrooms. All these approaches appeared highly effective in developing meaningful integration of authentic scientific inquiry, education research and assessment, and specific needs and settings of practitioners' classrooms.

While understanding students' prior knowledge, using effective approaches, and providing opportunities for interaction are necessary for successful transfer of authentic science to classrooms, they are not sufficient. Development of the learning ecology that makes this transfer possible requires a special kind of interaction and collaboration among practitioners, graduate students, scientists, and education faculty that results in the emergence of symbiotic learning communities. The sections below describe the nature of these interactions and the characteristics of collaboration within these communities.

Mutual Respect and Recognition of Collective Expertise

The success of SLCs was attributable, in part, to the recognition that all team members brought expertise and experience that directly contributed to the learning outcomes of everyone involved. The mutual respect among learning community members helped to form a collaborative learning environment that directly impacted practitioner learning and the development of SIFs.

The collaborative learning environment truly benefited all team members. The practitioners further developed their science (content) knowledge, as well as learning more about how to facilitate learning (pedagogical knowledge). Science faculty learned a great deal from the practitioners in terms of their dedication to and insights about teaching. Beyond that, science faculty were exposed to educational theory and assessment approaches that caused them to rethink and alter their own teaching. Many of the participating science faculty subsequently have become leaders and agents of change in reforming classroom teaching in their respective departments. They have conducted numerous seminars on their teaching innovations and actively mentored their peers and graduate students in effective pedagogy. Some have received external funding for research on teaching and learning in their classrooms.

Cooperation, Patience, and Building Bonds Among SLC Members

Collaboration for mutual benefit and the existence of bonds among participants were noticeable characteristics of successful SLCs that developed symbiotic relationships. For practitioners and education graduate students, much of the science content was relatively new. For the science graduate students, teaching and education content were relatively new. Furthermore, all of the participants were dealing with technology. These experiences brought most of the participants outside their comfort zone at times, which caused frustration. Patience both with the learning process and with one another became very important in pushing participants in new and unfamiliar directions. As an example, it was typical for one of the SLCs to spend the first half of their meetings as a group, either discussing their frameworks or being introduced to new content (Wu, Acheson, & Lafferty, 2005). In the second half of their meetings, participants were given time to work on their SIFs. Many times, participants spent time helping one of their community members rather than working on their own frameworks. For one of the practitioners who struggled at times with the technology, one participant regularly helped her and answered questions. She noted that he "has been real gracious." A science graduate student was helped by one of the practitioners, who explained education content to him; he described this practitioner as his "go-to-guy when I didn't understand the teaching, education thing."

Successful SLCs created opportunities for bonding among participants. Several communities had a dedicated laboratory with computers, and participants often came back to the laboratories in the evenings to work on assignments. During those afternoons and evenings, many bonds were forged among the members of the learning community. A participant recalled:

> We laughed together, collaborated on assignments, shared food and life stories as we maneuvered through the project's minefields. . . . As the weeks ended, we had listened, advised, cared and shared our projects and our lives, like a summer camp experience.

Future collaborations among the SLC members were also planned through these interactions.

Cooperation and Connection Between Science and Education Faculty

Cooperation between science and education faculty was necessary in order to help practitioners make meaningful connections between the science and pedagogy components of the inquiry experience. In some cases, joint conferences to discuss inquiry frameworks were conducted that included individual practitioners, a graduate student, a scientist, and an education faculty member. These meetings stood out as an effective approach for cooperation between science and education faculty. There were multiple lines of dialogue in these joint conferences: between the scientist and the practitioner on the scientific aspects of the inquiry, between the education faculty and the practitioner on the pedagogical aspects, and between the science and education faculty on the interplay of the two aspects. Graduate students also played an important role in these dialogues, acting as liaisons between faculty and practitioners. These conversations helped the practitioners make the connection between the science and education components and develop better SIFs and associated Practitioner Research Plans. The dialogues between the science and education faculty were also a great learning experience for faculty from both areas, and the observation of these interdisciplinary intellectual exchanges in action offered a rare education opportunity for the practitioners and graduate students. Furthermore, the discussions between science and education faculty brought better understanding of each other's fields, sparked interest in collaborative research in science education, and often led to sustained research collaboration among members of the SLCs (see e.g., Robledo, Wu, Knight, & Peterson, 2008; Simmons, Wu, Knight, & Lopez, 2006, 2008; Wu, Acheson, & Lafferty, 2005; Wu & Knight, 2006; Wu, Robledo, Knight, & Peterson, 2009; Wu et al., 2005).

The heterogeneous SLCs formed an integral component of the ITS Learning Ecology as it developed. The shared goal of all members of the communities, to bring current science into grade 7–16 classrooms, provided the impetus for the interdisciplinary and cross-boundary collaboration that rarely occurs in school–university joint endeavors. The need for multiple fields of expertise to accomplish the goal resulted in the development of mutual respect for and understanding of the complexity of the knowledge and skills of others. IT-based tools provided the framework for joint participation. SLCs consisting initially of independently operating experts transformed into symbiotic learning communities as they worked toward a common goal.

REFERENCES

Chapman, O., & Fiore, M. (2000). Calibrated peer review. *Journal of Interactive Instruction Development, 12*(3), 11–15.

Novak, J. D., & Gowin, D. B. (1984). *Learning how to learn*. New York: Cambridge University Press.

Robledo, D. C., Wu, X. B., Knight, S. L., & Peterson, C. A. (2008, August). *Effectiveness of calibrated peer review (CPR) on student learning in a web- and inquiry-based environment*. Paper presented at the annual meeting of the Ecological Society of America, Milwaukee, WI.

Runions, C. J., Brach, T., Kühner, S., & Hawes, C. (2006). Photoactivation of GFP reveals protein dynamics within the endoplasmic reticulum membrane. *Journal of Experimental Botany, 57*, 43–50.

Simmons, M., Wu, X. B., Knight, S. L., & Lopez, R. (2006, August). *GIS as a teaching tool in an undergraduate ecology laboratory: Assessing the use of GIS on students; motivation and conceptual knowledge*. Poster presentation at the annual meeting of the Ecological Society of America, Memphis, TN.

Simmons, M. E., Wu, X. B., Knight, S. L., & Lopez, R. R. (2008). Assessing the influence of field- and GIS-based inquiry on student attitude and conceptual knowledge in an undergraduate ecology lab. *CBE-Life Sciences Education, 7,* 338–345.

Wu, X. B., Acheson, G., & Lafferty, T. (2005, April). *Case study of the ITS landscape ecology science team as a community of learners.* In S. Knight & J. Schielack (Co-chairs), *Professional Development in Science and Mathematics through Communities of Learners.* Symposium conducted at the annual meeting of the American Educational Research Association, Montreal, Canada.

Wu, X. B., Xiao, Y., Knight, S. L., Li, J., Yin, C., Liu, F., Ao, C., Yue, C., Chang, D., Yang, Q., & Schielack, J. (2005, August). *Virtual Ecological Inquiry (VEI)—A virtual learning environment for ecological education and assessment research.* Paper presented at the annual meeting of the Ecological Society of America, Montreal, Canada.

Wu, X. B., & Knight, S. L. (2006, October). *Roles of actual and simulated data in IT- and inquiry-based ecology education: A case study with Virtual Ecological Inquiry (VEI).* Paper presented at the 20th International CODATA Conference, Beijing, China.

Wu, X. B., Robledo, D. C., Knight, S. L., & Peterson, C. A. (2009, April). *Inquiry-based eLearning in large ecology classes and its impact.* Paper presented at the 20th International Conference on College Teaching and Learning, Jacksonville, FL.

CHAPTER 9

Adaptation and Development of ITS Learning Ecology Participants: An Individual Perspective

Karen McNeal and Ruth Anderson

Adaptation is the change in living organisms that allows them to live successfully in an environment and to cope with environmental stresses and pressures. In a complex system, adaptation is supported by several characteristics, including (1) interactions between system components, (2) changes in system state over space and time, (3) unpredictable self-organization that leads to feedback producing the emergence of structure or patterns, (4) chaotic behavior, and (5) nonlinear dynamics (Herbert, 2006; McNeal, Miller, & Herbert, 2008; Sell, Herbert, Stuessy, & Schielack, 2006). In ecology, these behaviors are explained through the term *ecological resilience*, which is defined as the amount of disturbance that an ecosystem can handle without changing its self-organized processes and structures (Holling, 1973). These behaviors are important for the system to function correctly and for the system to persist without detriment in order to fulfill its purpose. Adaptation or adaptive capacity describes the many stable states that an ecosystem can undergo to maintain its resilience to external pressures (Gunderson, 2000).

In this chapter we revisit populations of individuals within the Information Technology in Science (ITS) Learning Ecology and explore some of the ways they adapted to survive the changes to their environment as it evolved. Specifically, we examine the extent to which the three principal populations in the ITS Learning Ecology (grade 7–16 practitioners, university faculty, and graduate students) underwent adaptation and change as a result of the synergistic inquiry experiences. Who adapted and in what ways? What seemed to be the environmental triggers that prompted the changes? To what extent did the unique characteristics of the project lead to the need for certain groups of individuals to adapt more than others? Drawing on research and evaluation sources, we focus largely on the first three of the parameters mentioned above: interactions, changes, and emergence of patterns (i.e., emergent properties that each group exhibited as a result of their interactions with other groups and their ability to adapt over time).

As we examine the interactions among these populations, we make inferences based on a variety of data sources collected over the life of the project, including surveys, interviews, focus groups, and observational data. As we consider each population's patterns of change and attempt to compare these across populations, we refer to a common set of four categories:

1. *Knowledge,* or understanding of education theory and research, science research, K–12 science inquiry, the nature of secondary science education, and technologies related to science learning and teaching
2. *Attitude,* or confidence in teaching, using technology in the classroom, conducting inquiry in the classroom, conducting science research, and conducting education research
3. *Professional practice,* including integrating science and education in research, using technology in the classroom, using inquiry in the classroom, and collaboration—with communities both within and outside the ITS Learning Ecology
4. *Role,* or extent and type of engagement in science education within and outside of the ITS Learning Ecology.

OVERVIEW OF THE POPULATIONS IN THE ITS LEARNING ECOLOGY

Practitioners were the largest group involved in the project, but they also had the most consistent turnover during the life of the ITS Learning Ecology. The practitioners represented a variety of types of instructional settings, from large inner-city urban schools with many science teachers in one hall to very small rural districts with one science teacher. This diversity in instructional setting also introduced a strong component of diversity in the grade 7–16 students that participated in the ITS Learning Ecology activities through the involvement of these practitioners. (See Chapter 1 for more details.)

University faculty constituted the most consistently engaged group, experiencing relatively little turnover during the 6 years. This group, made up of faculty members from both education and science departments, designed and facilitated the synergistic inquiry experiences each year. Science teams and education faculty signed on for each cohort, but many stayed on for more than one cohort.

Graduate students from education and science represented a group that worked in between faculty and practitioners. At the start of the project, most of them came directly from either the education department or one of the participating science departments. With time, however, a growing number of the graduate students emerged from the population of practitioners. Since the practitioners were recruited with an eye to increasing the diversity of science education leadership, bringing these individuals into the group of full-time graduate students enhanced the diversity of that group.

The Practitioners

The grade 7–16 practitioners were recipients of the program content. They were the students of the ITS Learning Ecology, which provided them with a unique professional development experience during two summers and the expectation of implementing changes when they returned to their home instructional environments during each of the post-summer academic years. Although their primary role as learner remained constant, they soon acquired a secondary role of catalyst of change for other groups within the ITS Learning Ecology.

Interactions. Each summer, practitioners would spend 3 weeks at a university working daily with university faculty in both science and education, learning about and conducting authentic scientific research, and using technologies rarely available to them in the public education system. Additionally, they would read and discuss the latest educational research, write papers, and conduct presentations. These were not elements of the typical teacher professional development experience they had previously encountered. Their interactions with fellow practitioners, graduate students, and faculty across science, technology, engineering, and mathematics (STEM) disciplines and within educational research were intense during the summer. However, once back in their home environments, the practitioners were little influenced by the ITS Learning Ecology environment, which, as we see in the next section, affected the kind and degree of changes that they experienced as a group.

Patterns in Adaptation. Figure 9.1 summarizes the changes exhibited by the practitioners in the ITS Learning Ecology. The arrows represent the interpretation of numerous programmatic data sets, including sample interviews, internal evaluation surveys, and follow-up surveys throughout the duration of the program. Exposure to authentic inquiry and practitioner research in the program gave practitioners greater knowledge about conducting science and education research, as reported via self-reflections. As one practitioner noted,

Figure 9.1. Qualitative Illustration Summarizing the Adaptation of the Practitioners

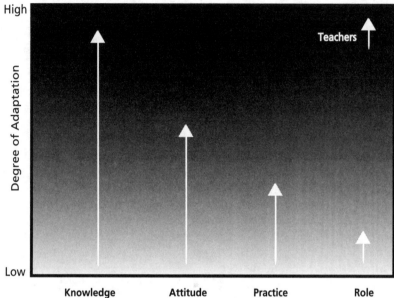

It's always . . . good to get together with a science researcher because it reminds me of what it was like to be out in the field and actually conduct the experiment. . . . It's good for me to remember that you don't know what the answer is when you go into science [experiments].

Also, their attitudes were highly affected in the areas of confidence in conducting science and education research and in using technology and inquiry in the classroom. The daily use of technology in the program, the modeled inquiry lessons, and the development of their own inquiry- and technology-rich classroom implementation provided the practitioners confidence to conduct inquiry and use technology in their own classrooms. For example, one practitioner said, "I didn't use to use any technology and [ITS] has got me past that barrier." Not surprisingly, the practitioners' sense of self-efficacy in teaching in general was not greatly affected—likely because, as experienced educators, they were already highly confident coming into the project.

Changes related to professional practice and collaboration (role) were limited among the practitioners. As a result of their individually developed Student Inquiry Frameworks (SIFs), many practitioners reported an increased use of technology and inquiry or broader collaboration as they partnered with scientists and other grade 7–16 practitioners in the ITS Learning Ecology. Several practitioners made remarks such as, "I have given up more control to the kids. . . . I've been thinking how can I help other science teachers on my campus." Nevertheless, there is little evidence of such changes lasting beyond their individual implementation. In other words, there was no true adaptation aligned with the ITS Learning Ecology environment. Likely this was due to the practitioners' intermittent and otherwise limited contact with that environment. They were exposed to the ITS Learning Ecology only for short intervals during the summer workshops, and then they exited the environment to return to their home schools during the academic year. With so much less exposure to the ITS Learning Ecology than the other two groups of individuals, it is not surprising that practitioners experienced the least amount of change in role and practice.

The University Faculty

Science and education faculty began with separate but parallel responsibilities as content experts, summer institute instructors, and facilitators of the ITS Learning Ecology objectives. As the environment developed, however, their engagement became more integrated. This integrated engagement also expanded to include an increased level of collaboration between science- and education-focused objectives and between faculty and the other members of the ITS Learning Ecology (practitioners and graduate students).

Interactions. As suggested above, interactions between faculty and members of other ITS Learning Ecology populations became more frequent and complex over time. Early in the development of the ITS Learning Ecology, there was minimal contact between science and education faculty or even between faculty and graduate students who were not from the same academic departments. Practitioners, on the other hand, interacted intensely with both faculty and graduate students during the summers, and their demand for a more integrated and congruent summer experience put pressure on both science and education faculty to change their pattern of interaction with one another. Consequently, by the second year of the project, education and science faculty began to interact more. At first, these interactions began as formal events—planned collaborations with the shared goal of improving the learning experiences of practitioners. Eventually, however, the cross-discipline interactions began to occur more spontaneously and for other motivations, such as sharing responsibility for graduate students, shared research, or even new proposals for science education projects.

Patterns in Adaptation. Figure 9.2 summarizes the changes exhibited by the university faculty. Just as the science and education faculty began as separate, but similar, groups in the ITS Learning Ecology, so their patterns in adaptation were distinct from, but in some ways similar to, each other.

Figure 9.2. Qualitative Illustration Summarizing the Adaptation of the University Faculty

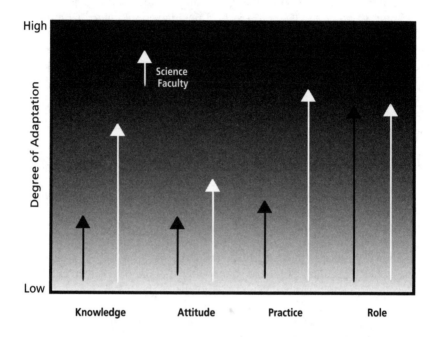

In most areas, the two groups of faculty showed parallel patterns of change. However, as initial *outsiders* to educational research and secondary science education, the pressure for the science faculty to adapt was more acute than for the education faculty. Using a 5-point Likert Scale assessment (with $p < 0.05$ on a Wilcoxon rank sum), education faculty did not indicate any areas of statistically significant change, while science faculty indicated statistically significant change in several areas.

Science faculty reported a gain in knowledge through greater understanding of what learning means and how people learn. In addition, science faculty felt that they were more knowledgeable about what practitioners need to know in order to be prepared to teach in grades 7–12, about what the college of education faculty do to foster practitioner development, and about the pedagogical approaches and assessment techniques used in teaching science in grades 7–12.

Science faculty's increased knowledge was accompanied by a change in attitude through a new appreciation of inquiry and a desire to incorporate it into their classrooms. They expressed increased interest in changing the way undergraduates experience science in their courses and were more concerned with changing science education-related policies and practices in their departments.

In general, the science faculty reported and exhibited the greatest degree of change across the board, but most prominently in the area of professional practice. Science faculty, for example, began to integrate science education research into their research foci. Some even began to guide their graduate students in conducting science and science education research during their dissertations; others published papers on the state of education in their specific discipline. A few reported changing the structure of undergraduate courses to include more inquiry and interaction. In one science department, a participating scientist even took on the responsibility of head of undergraduate courses. In the same department, he and his colleagues joined with education faculty on doctoral committees. Some science departments now consider publications in science education journals for promotion requirements. At least one scientist said he was introducing graduate student learning communities (as opposed to simply one-on-one talks with the professor).

In terms of role development, both science and science education faculty created collaborations that previously did not exist within and between groups. For instance, partnerships between education and science faculty led to the submission and subsequent award of several new federally funded projects. Furthermore, both science and science education faculty participated in dissertation committees across disciplines, with education faculty serving on science committees and vice versa. In general, science faculty reported a greater level of collaboration and comfort with education faculty (though maintaining a greater respect for the work of their fellow scientists).

The Graduate Students

The handful of graduate students involved in the first cohort began as participants alongside the grade 7–16 practitioners. Each graduate student participated in the summer institute and implemented an SIF during the academic year.

At the onset of the program, the majority of the graduate students involved were from education disciplines. Only a few had distinct responsibilities as liaisons between the science and education communities, which were working separately. As the project evolved and more science graduate students were brought on, they, too, became liaisons. Soon after, however, the liaison position evolved into a position of leadership and co-teaching. No longer just support staff, graduate students began to lead summer institute sessions and co-teach content. As such, they became integral players in the overall teaching and learning process of the ITS Learning Ecology. They were co-facilitators of practitioner and graduate student participation in the Science Learning Communities (SLCs) and in the development of the SIFs; and they became communicators and interpreters of science and education culture, terminology, and research methods.

Interactions. The graduate students' changing responsibilities within the ITS Learning Ecology had an impact on the nature and extent of their interactions with other groups of participants. The addition of science graduate students as members of the ITS Learning Ecology meant that there was a greater level of exchange and collaboration between science and education departments at the graduate student level. As helpers and eventually co-facilitators of the synergistic inquiry experience, the graduate students interacted closely with both university faculty and practitioners. And by being paired as facilitators, the graduate students experienced particularly intense cross-discipline interaction. Perhaps not surprisingly, a social networking study conducted later in the project (see Figure 7.2 in Chapter 7) revealed the graduate students as the principal nodes of communication and interaction within the ITS Learning Ecology.

Patterns in Adaptation. The graduate students were the most dynamic group of participants in the ITS Learning Ecology, experiencing high degrees of change in all categories, including extreme adaptation with regard to their role, as shown in Figure 9.3. As a result of their experiences, graduate students in both science and education exhibited well-developed leadership skills in the facilitation of professional development for practitioners, participated in a strong learning and research community actively focused on the learning and teaching of science, reported positive opportunities and changes in their graduate studies and in their future careers in science and education, and recognized and appreciated their understanding of participation in the various groups within the ITS Learning Ecology. Like their faculty counterparts, however, the science and science education graduate students did not adapt or develop in unison, for several possible reasons. For example, the science graduate students were immersed in a *foreign* environment, making the need to adapt more necessary for them than for their science education peers. As one education graduate student described it: "The whole [experience] was in our comfort zone." A couple of cited benefits included "a better understanding of the education research literature—how to read research" and an increased understanding of interdisciplinary collaboration: "interacting with scientists . . . becoming aware of how isolated education is from the science field." The culture, the terminology, the content, and the context of the ITS Learning Ecology were all examples of specific factors that made it necessary for the science graduate students to change quickly.

The graduate students' knowledge development is reflected in their understanding of key components of the program. Science graduate students showed the greatest development with regard to understanding education research and theory, understanding inquiry, and understanding grade 7–16 education. They showed moderate development in the areas of understanding science research and technology. Education graduate students showed the greatest development in understanding science research and technology, moderate development in understanding inquiry and education theory and research, and little development in

Figure 9.3. Qualitative Illustration Summarizing the Adaptation of the Graduate Students

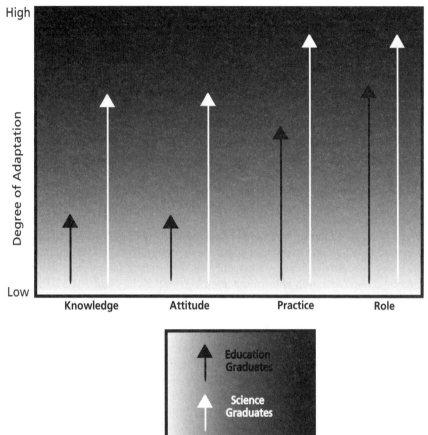

understanding grade 7–16 education. One of the major reasons for this difference in development between the two groups is that the science graduate students had never been exposed to the terminology and literature used in the learning ecology. For instance, terms such as *epistemology, cognition, metacognition, conceptual and mental model, backwards design, inquiry cycle, mixed methods,* and other routinely used education vocabulary were not familiar to the science graduate students. The challenge became to become bilingual (in both science and education) very quickly, as expressed by a science graduate student:

> It's just being able to talk both languages—is a really strong tribute to our being exposed—not just working together, but our being exposed to the dual environment . . . if we go to a science department that is also interested in education, we can also speak the education language. If we go

to an education department and they want to work with scientists, we can speak the science language. And prove and show that we've worked with other scientists and educators before so we've already been able to establish [relationships] and can collaborate . . . which is always important.

On the other hand, many of the education graduate students had previous degrees in science disciplines, and although they tended to show improvement in understanding science research, they did not have the same vocabulary issues the science graduate students encountered. Additionally, many of the education graduate students had experience teaching prior to enrolling in graduate school and therefore did not show pronounced development in understanding in this area. Both groups had little to no prior exposure to implementing inquiry or technology in the classroom, so development of their understanding was generally noted in these areas.

As a result of their exposure to the ITS Learning Ecology and their changing responsibilities, the attitudes of both groups of graduate students were affected. The science graduate students showed the greatest increases in their confidence in regard to teaching, conducting education research, and conducting inquiry in the classroom. Moderate increases were indicated in their confidence about conducting science research and using technology in the classroom. In contrast, the education graduate students showed the greatest increases in their confidence about conducting science research and using technology in the classroom. Moderate increases were indicated in their confidence about conducting education research and conducting inquiry in the classroom. Little to no increase was noted in regard to their confidence in teaching. These trends can be explained by the fact that the science graduate students came with little teaching in their backgrounds, whereas many of the education graduate students had more previous exposure to teaching. However, many of the education graduate students did not have extended exposure to conducting science research or using technology as did the science graduate students. Both groups had little experience conducting inquiry in the classroom and therefore initially had low confidence in this area.

The development of the graduate students' professional practice was also greatly influenced by their exposure to the ITS Learning Ecology. Most notably, the science graduate students' integration of science and education into their research was the practice most impacted. Many of the science graduate students completed dissertations that included research in their science field as well as in the science education arena where the two efforts became synergistic. Additionally, their collaboration outside their own group was drastically influenced in cases in which they included education faculty on their dissertation committees and collaborated with them on journal publications and conference presentations. Both science and education graduate students adapted their practices in using technology and inquiry in the classroom, largely due to their SIFs, which resulted from the synergistic inquiry experiences. Both groups also seemed to show increased collaboration within and between their groups, as a result of belonging to the ITS Learning Ecology. For instance, graduate students in education, engineering, geology, biology, geography, and wildlife and fisheries departments took courses together, completed projects together, and at times even published papers and conducted professional presentations together—all because they were members of the same learning ecology.

Due to both personal and academic ties (e.g., between science departments and the college of education; between practitioners and the ITS Learning Ecology), the graduate students evidenced a high level of adaptation by effectively taking on the role of bridge builders among the various communities participating in the project. As these future scientists and education researchers explored the relationship between science and the science of learning, they grappled with issues that challenged communication and understanding between their academic cultures of origin. The mutual understanding and respect that they built as fellow graduate students will likely remain with them as they settle within science and education departments around the country and around the world. This diverse group of emerging scientists and education specialists had the opportunity to influence one another's research, thinking, and practice with regard to science learning. Science graduates claimed that their focus on the science of learning "made them better scientists" and expressed appreciation for being able to "speak both languages" (that of science and education). Specific comments from one science graduate included, "I have a better understanding of how to conduct scientific inquiry in my own research. I've discovered that the research process can be transferred between science education and science disciplines." Another student reported a different but valuable learning experience: "I'm not certain it has made me a better science researcher. If anything, I do think that I am better able to explain what I do. So yes, from a communication perspective, it's made me better."

HYBRID OR NEW BREED?

This chapter summarizes the various responses of populations in the ITS Learning Ecology as a result of the complex and dynamic nature of the social organization. The science faculty were more willing to engage in effective inquiry pedagogies in their classrooms, and they greatly valued prioritizing education efforts and related research in their own fields and institutions. Many of the practitioners became science leaders in their home institutes and resident science education experts who conduct professional development in their home schools. However, graduate students were the most transformed by the ITS experience.

Do the graduate students who emerged from the ITS Learning Ecology for science education leadership, with its (perhaps unique) view of science education in which both science and the science of learning and teaching are valued and applied, constitute a *hybrid* or a *new breed* of higher education science educator? Wherever they end up participating in K–20 education, they will do so with a better understanding of one another's academic cultures of origin. In the K–12 world, this means science education leaders better skilled in translating authentic science into the pre-college classroom. As scientists at the university level, these individuals, with their greater understanding of the academic culture of education and better knowledge of the research on how people learn, could be important agents of change within academia, where the cultural divide between science and science education is often broad.

These results of participation in the ITS Learning Ecology support the basis of a model for future modifications to science graduate student programs. The creation of a new generation of scientists who are trained with specializations in science education and are knowledgeable in teaching and mentoring, education theory and practice, and science and science education research is an outcome that could be mirrored in the development of similar programs. These outcomes could provide the necessary skills for graduate student success in academic careers where traditional training programs may fail. The production of strong science leaders who are passionate and knowledgeable about education and can communicate in both science and education communities and respective cultures, providing the bridge between disciplines, could be yet another outcome of such a program. Perhaps it is now time to rethink how science graduate student programs are designed and to employ a new model that encourages some of the many disciplinary crosscutting and innovative aspects of the ITS Learning Ecology.

An answer to the question "How can the PhD meet the needs of the 21st century?" is being sought nationwide (Good & Lane, 1994; Nyquist, 2002). Recent reports examining the preparedness of the PhD graduate for employment have identified gaps between the focus of doctoral programs and the work actually expected upon completion; specifically, graduate students are reportedly not prepared to take on faculty responsibilities, especially with regard to teaching (Adams, 2002; Gaff, 2002). Gaff (2002) reports that less than half of the 32,600 respondents involved in a nationwide graduate web survey agreed that teaching assistants were appropriately trained before entering the classroom, and less than 40% indicated that teaching assistants were adequately supervised to improve their teaching skills. Similarly, a call for severe change in faculty mentorship of graduate students has been made in order to promote a student's readiness for faculty positions that emphasize teaching (Adams, 2002). Several national initiatives have been implemented to rectify the demands for change (the National Science Foundation's *Preparing Future Faculty Project*; the Pew-funded *Re-Envisioning the Ph.D. Project*; the *Responsive Ph.D. Fellowship*, funded by the Woodrow Wilson National Fellowship Foundation; and the *Carnegie Initiative on the Doctorate*, a fellowship funded by the Carnegie Foundation). The common threads in all of these efforts are teaching competency, preparedness to be a leader, and ability to evaluate others' learning, among others (Nyquist, 2002). A program such as the one resulting in the ITS Learning Ecology has the ability to support such calls for doctoral reform through the experiences it provides for its science graduate students.

Although all populations adapted to varying degrees in response to the external stresses placed on them, the science graduate students were the most resilient to the changes in the environment, where the resulting modified behaviors produced a higher level of functioning both within the learning ecology and in other facets of their graduate work and careers. The strength of this outcome was not expected at the onset of the project, but the flexible design structure of the ITS Learning Ecology enabled this particular population to thrive and evolve into a new breed of science education leaders. It is our hope that the learning ecology presented in this book can be a model for future projects in which the development of science education leadership as a component of a high-quality science graduate student is a desired outcome.

REFERENCES

Adams, K. A. (2002). *What colleges and universities want in new faculty.* Washington, DC: Association of American Colleges and Universities.

Gaff, J. G. (2002, November/December). Preparing future faculty and doctoral education. *Educational Researcher,* pp. 63–66. Washington, DC: Association of American Colleges and Universities.

Good, M. L., & Lane, N. F. (1994). Producing the finest scientists and engineers for the 21st century. *Science, 266,* 741–743.

Gunderson, L. H. (2000). Ecological resilience—In theory and application. *Annual Review of Ecology and Systematics, 31,* 425–439.

Hamilton, S. F. (1983). The social side of schooling: Ecological studies of classrooms and schools. *The Elementary School Journal, 83,* 313–334.

Herbert, B. E. (2006). Student understanding of complex Earth systems (Special Paper No. 413). In C. A. Manduca & D. W. Mogk (Eds.), *Geologists think and learn about the Earth* (pp. 95–103). Boulder, CO: Geological Society of America.

Holling, C. S. (1973). Resilience and stability of ecological systems. *Annual Review of Ecology and Systematics, 4,* 1–23.

McNeal, K. S., Miller, H. R., & Herbert, B. E. (2008). The effect of using inquiry and multiple representations on introductory geology students' conceptual model development of coastal eutrophication. *Journal of Geoscience Education, 56,* 201–211.

Nyquist, J. D. (2002, November/December). The PhD: A tapestry of change. *Educational Researcher,* pp. 12–20.

Sell, K. S., Herbert, B. E., Stuessy, C. & Schielack, J. (2006). Supporting student conceptual model development of complex earth systems through the use of multiple representations and inquiry. *Journal of Geoscience Education, 54,* 396–407.

Part IV

CONCLUSION: LESSONS LEARNED

Emergent behaviors, like games, are all about living within boundaries defined by the rules, but also using that space to create something greater than the sum of its parts (from S. Johnson in *Emergence: The connected lives of ants, brains, cities and software*, published by Scribner, New York, NY, 2001, p. 181).

Part IV presents the lessons learned from the ITS Learning Ecology. Chapter 10 describes the critical components of the complex environment needed to support an IT-based learning ecology for science education leadership. It draws from research in organizational theory to identify components critical to creating an integrated program that promotes the development of a productive, interdependent learning ecology.

Critical Components of an IT-Based Learning Ecology Model for Science Education Leadership

Ruth Anderson and Jim Minstrell

The Information Technology in Science (ITS) Learning Ecology was an experiment to discover ways to improve science education through the intermingling of grade 7–16 practitioners and university science and science education faculty (or, as some skeptically described it, "add scientists and stir"). There was no preconceived notion of *centerness* when funding began. Implicit in the program was an expectation of *cultural change* in the participating institutions of higher education (IHEs), which in turn might promote greater alignment of grade 7–16 science education. Such experiments in social engineering have been going on for the past few decades in various disciplines, mostly falling under the umbrella term of *school–university partnerships* (see, e.g., Sirotnik & Goodlad, 1988). This label, however, does not accurately convey the complexity of these multicultural endeavors. For example, we tend to emphasize the distinctions between grade 7–12 and higher education environments, while often ignoring the diversity that exists within each of those large professional communities. Yet whether the collaboration is interinstitutional or interdepartmental, it necessarily involves multiple professional cultures and requires the negotiation of cultural boundaries.

The first chapter in this book introduced the analogy of a learning ecology to describe the community of scientists and education specialists from which the ITS Learning Ecology model—and a new breed of science educator—emerged. In this chapter, we look at key elements involved in the evolution of the ITS Learning Ecology from a loose confederation of diverse individuals engaged in parallel play to a collaborative and productive interdisciplinary network. We do so through two different frameworks. The first draws on the organizational

development literature that is commonly used to describe educational collaborations; the second draws on some principles of complexity science as recently
applied to learning environments. While we feel that both frameworks convey
some noteworthy lessons learned from this particular project, the second seems
to raise important questions and implications for research and evaluation of the
emergent complex systems that are educational partnerships.

We, as independent external evaluators, draw on 6 years of evaluation data
particular to this project as well as several years of experience with similar educational programs. The examples and associated lessons learned come out of
activities such as interviews, observations, surveys, and focus groups conducted
with a range of individuals and groups from the participating community (i.e.,
education and science faculty, graduate students, grade 7–16 practitioners, and
project leadership).

CREATING THE COMPLEX SYSTEM

The ITS Learning Ecology exhibited the following key components that contributed to its development as a complex system: having the right people participate,
providing a common place for interactions to take place while developing a common history, and creating a culture apart from others that existed.

The Right People

People and relationships will likely always be at the core of any successful
collaborative venture.

> Human relationships are critically important to the health of an information ecology
> as they make the various interactions and interdependencies possible. Relationships,
> more than information, determine how problems are solved or opportunities
> exploited. These social networks of human ties of trust and reciprocity generate much
> of the capital on which the participants can leverage. (Looi, 2001, p. 14)

But how does one determine who will be the *right people* at the onset of a
project? In the case of the integrated, interdisciplinary Science Learning Communities (SLCs), it was surprising to discover that it was not the experts in science
teacher education but rather the intelligent novices that proved the best fit for
the project's emerging model of professional development (Bruer, 1993). Qualities like flexibility, comfort with ambiguity, curiosity, and the ability to reflect, be
self-critical, and change course based on evidence were all important attributes.
These attributes, coupled with commitment to success, turned out to be more
important than prior experience with teacher professional development.

In the first set of SLCs, for example, a couple of groups were led by scientists or science educators who had had extensive experience designing and leading workshops and summer programs for grade 7–12 science teachers. These teams came in with their own clear vision of what needed to be done and were ready from the start to deliver their own version of a blended experience of science and education to their practitioners. The teams were highly independent and did not seem to value the emerging model of professional development. Keeping to themselves and making few attempts to collaborate with the education faculty or other SLCs, they also tended to be highly critical of the education portion of the experience. They expressed concern that there was not more consistency across SLCs in terms of learning goals and products and were not shy about pointing out what appeared to be flaws in the design of the project. Their criticisms were not groundless — especially in the early stages of the project — but because they essentially acted in isolation from the larger group, the contributions of these professional development experts did not become a part of the ITS Learning Ecology environment. Not surprisingly, such individuals did not choose to remain in the project.

On the other hand, the research scientists without previous experience in teacher education seemed to fare better in the SLCs. Although they often began with pre-conceived ideas about grade 7–12 teachers and their needs, they did not have set ideas about *how* teachers should be learning. This may explain in part why they appeared more willing to experiment with the ways in which they shared science content with the practitioner members of their community. In *Schools for Thought*, Bruer (1993) notes,

> In the early 1980's researchers turned their attention to other apparent features of expert performance. They noticed that there were intelligent novices — people who learned new fields and solved novel problems more expertly than most, regardless of how much domain-specific knowledge they possessed. Intelligent novices controlled and monitored their thought processes and made use of general, domain-independent strategies and skills where appropriate. (p. 52)

Considering themselves learners rather than experts in the area of teacher education, they did not generally attempt to dictate what should be happening. This does not mean they were not critical of what they perceived to be problems or obstacles in the project. However, these "intelligent novices" (Bruer, 1993) generally seemed to be more concerned with the needs of the practitioners in their own SLCs and less with how the larger project should be developing. And while later groups also tended to be very independent, the majority also welcomed collaboration with — and feedback from — the education faculty as they adjusted what they were doing within their specific SLCs. In retrospect, they approached their new work like scientists or engineers, making changes in what they did based on what they determined worked or did not work.

This does not imply that experienced participants are less qualified. However, with experience come understandings, beliefs, and practices accepted as normal and desirable in one's environment that may be difficult to overcome in the interest of creating something new and innovative. Just as students with the strongest mental models or preconceptions about particular concepts tend to have the hardest time overcoming those preconceptions (Bransford, Brown, & Cocking, 2000), so it may be that individuals with very firm preconceptions of what and how teachers need to enhance their science knowledge and teaching skills have more difficulty overcoming those preconceptions and adopting a different approach to teacher professional development. Without too many pre-conceived notions about what should be, there may be greater comfort with ambiguity and change.

Common Place and History

The participating faculty and graduate students of the project were members of the same university. The significance of this common location should not be underestimated. Interinstitutional collaborations pose substantial challenges in terms of developing practical logistics and building community among partners. The common location for this project facilitated such operational essentials as resource distribution and scheduling. The alignment of research agendas and institutional processes and procedures (including human subjects requirements and reward and financial system) was also greatly facilitated by proximity.

Common location also seemed to contribute significantly to the stability of the ITS Learning Ecology, where there was surprisingly little turnover in faculty or graduate student involvement. In his research on partnerships, Kingsley has observed that successful collaborations are facilitated by employing groups of people who have an established positive working history (Kingsley & Waschak, 2005). Beyond operational logistics, a common location facilitated meetings—especially among those faculty members who did not readily meet through their departments of origin. The opportunity and purpose for coming together face-to-face (i.e., designing and planning for the summer inquiry experience) prompted the establishment of at least informal relationships. Some of these relationships were then formalized through jointly supporting and mentoring graduate students or collaborating on research within the realm of the project and beyond. In the case of individual SLCs, some of the most successful consisted of individuals with established personal relationships—whether or not they had previously worked together. On the other hand, looser associations of scientists, working together for the first time and without previous personal ties, did not necessarily result in the same type of experience.

Cohesive teams from a common department had greater potential for influencing change because they provided the critical mass of participation needed for the dissemination of innovations and collaboration. This was the case in some science departments where several key faculty members were involved in the project. After making adjustments to their instruction of practitioners during a synergistic inquiry experience, those SLC members collaborated further, working to apply what they were learning to some of their undergraduate courses. One research scientist eventually took on the departmental role of managing the undergraduate program in order to have a greater influence on the design and delivery of those courses. In two other science departments, faculty lobbied to include an education emphasis in their tenure and promotion portfolios, based on work that had come out of their experience with the ITS Learning Ecology, and ultimately succeeded. In contrast, no such changes occurred among the participating grade 7–12 practitioner population—largely, we suspect, because the practitioners were the sole representatives of their respective schools. There was no tipping point of ITS Learning Ecology influence that could occur.

Working Toward a Culture Apart

The previous section highlighted the advantage of starting with a common organizational culture (i.e., a single university campus), but this does not mean that the distinctions of subcultures within the parent organization can be glossed over. In discussing the process of change in school–university collaboration, Slater effectively describes the multicultural nature of school collaborations and the inherent challenge of creating a new common space for the collaboration to happen. Slater (2001) notes that change is slow and artificial, competing with ingrained practices, and that change often requires that "a new culture or a variation of the cultural milieu be produced" (p. 21). She illustrates the development toward a *culture apart* through "Zones of Organizational Involvement" (p. 14). Each zone is characterized by both fixed and transitional behaviors as a way of illustrating a fluid process in which members may move forward and backward from their original culture to the new culture and back again—a sort of zig-zag path from coordination and cooperation to full collaboration. It is not difficult to see the ITS Learning Ecology's own trajectory through Slater's framework.

Zone 1, for example, finds its members still firmly rooted in the practices, norms, and values of their parent organizations (e.g., academic departments) even though their work may be coordinated with that of others. Transitional behaviors leading into the next zone include cooperating with others within the new culture (i.e., new organization), forming new alliances, and even taking individual risks. Zone 1 seems to characterize the first few years of the ITS Learning Ecology's organizational state. The early community, not yet a culture apart, was dominated by the professional cultures of science education researchers and education specialists. Representatives from these two departments made up the leadership team and discussed longer-term goals for the project. Graduate students, not yet *products* of the synergistic inquiry experiences, were strongly rooted in their home departments of science or education and were very attached to the advisers who had funded them through the new program. Similarly, science and education faculty contributed separately to the inquiry experience and rarely overlapped physically during the 3-week professional development event. Nevertheless, within the environment of the inquiry experience, individual scientists, eager to be effective with their practitioners, were beginning to experiment with new ways of approaching instruction.

Slater (2001) labels Zone 2 the Danger Zone. It is a stage where members begin to exhibit behaviors distinct from those of the parent organization and participate in intergroup processes. The task-oriented collaborations at this point may be fragile—perhaps in part because they are viewed as temporary. Transitional behaviors leading toward Zone 3 include intergroup collaboration and thinking that become the norm for their work in the new environments (i.e., parent organization practices no longer dominate). In addition, individual parent organizations may be altered.

By Year 3 of the project, the ITS Learning Ecology had entered Zone 2. A unique identity was clearly emerging—especially among the graduate students, who were now referring to themselves as graduate students affiliated with the ITS Learning Ecology rather than affiliated with one specific science department. These students, who began as SLC participants, had moved on to assist in—and were now full facilitators of—some aspects of the synergistic inquiry experience for practitioners. In their academic studies, science and science education graduate students were thinking together and affecting one another's research. Their collaboration foreshadowed the possibility of change in the established professional cultures in science and education. Especially within this group, an ITS Learning Ecology identity was forming.

While the interdisciplinary collaborations of faculty still largely took place around the summer component of the synergistic inquiry experience, graduate students had begun to work together year-round. Nevertheless, there appeared to be movement across zones among the faculty as well. Many science faculty for the first time began to conduct education research. Education specialists began scrutinizing the similarities and differences between inquiry as it occurs in the various fields of science and the inquiry of reformed science classrooms. In a few cases, scientists and education specialists collaborated on research projects. There were also some examples of ITS Learning Ecology influence on departments of origin. At least two faculty members reported that they had "permanently changed" the way they mentored their graduate students based on what they had learned through the ITS Learning Ecology experience. In one of the science departments, two research scientists who were putting together their tenure portfolios lobbied for—and were granted—recognition of their educational research among their publications. While this did not become departmental policy, it did set a new precedent within the rewards structure of their departments. These examples appeared as seeds of change planted in both individuals and their departments of origin, highlighting the ITS Learning Ecology's movement to the *transitional* border of Zone 2.

The third and final zone of Slater's framework describes a fully functioning independent organization where the members are thinking like a community and engaged in both future-oriented learning and problem solving. Members of the new environment have permanently adopted behaviors aligned with the new community, and behaviors that emerged from the Danger Zone became the norm in the parent organizations. Although the ITS Learning Ecology did not appear to reach this state in its 6 years as a community, some of the community members did exhibit some Zone 3 traits. For example, several members have since pursued funding for other science education projects, using the Integrated Professional Development Model (see Chapter 4) as the basis of their new projects. Another example is a scientist/education researcher team that initially came together for SLC-based research and ended up collaborating on other research during and beyond the project. Still another example is a pair of scientists who, largely as a result of their ITS Learning Ecology experience, have taken on greater responsibility for undergraduate learning in their department and have instituted design changes based on what they learned from participation in the project about learner cognition and effective learning environments.

Creating a Culture Apart

Slater's (2001) Zones of Organizational Development are useful in describing the course of development of community, but they do not provide reasons for that development. The ITS Learning Ecology provided the opportunity for individuals from diverse departmental cultures to come together in a low-stakes environment (i.e., ultimately temporary and independent of their home department) to experiment together and individually with their thinking and research related to science learning and teaching. Looking back on the work in their SLC, faculty and graduate students identified several components that allowed the development of a culture apart from their home department cultures—one that tried and often managed to level the playing field for participating members. They also found that traditional and naive thinking about science education could blend in an effort to create something new. We look briefly at some of those ways in which cultural boundaries were negotiated in the ITS Learning Ecology in order to create a culture apart for the participating community.

Accessible Language/Common Language. Increased collaboration among diverse groups increases the need for expanded modes of expression since "[t]he limits of my language mean the limits of my world" (Wittgenstein,

1918, 56). Collaboration is a way to engage a wider range of ideas and perceptions while retaining meaning for all. Reflecting on an early stage of the project, the director expressed the ITS Learning Ecology's struggle with this task:

> We knew when we started that we had different languages. We tried to develop a common language. As a result, we ended up doing [our] business in a language outside any domain. The education people didn't see cognition [learning terms] and the scientists didn't see research terms. . . . By design or default we had to incorporate a way of translating things back into our own languages.

Through our evaluation work, we noticed a steady change in the use of language among the faculty and graduate students. At first there was a self-conscious use of terminology from one another's domains and, over time, a deliberate use of terms to express themselves. It seemed that as the terms gained meaning, they became useful tools. We noted this particularly among scientists and science graduate students who—at first sarcastically, later apologetically, and finally purposefully— came to use such terms as *scaffolding, learner-centered, metacognition,* or *problem-based inquiry* to explain what they were doing with practitioners. Eventually, they even used these terms in their own classrooms and education-related research. Similarly, among education faculty and graduate students, there was increased reference to specific scientific research and increased care taken in using nuanced vocabulary around aspects of scientific inquiry. Not surprisingly, it seemed that the graduate students (science and science education alike) most readily adopted and became fluent in the use of a common language. They seemed to easily incorporate it into their conversations with practitioners and faculty as well as into their research projects.

Most community members commenting on the development of ITS Learning Ecology language noted the importance of making it inclusive and not favoring any one parent organization (i.e., academic department). As one faculty member put it,

> The goal is really to give up your identity . . . and meet others on a leveled plane. [The challenge is] how to feel you're not diminishing your academic identity by being able to clearly communicate to people outside your group.

What was the catalyst for the emergence of common language? At least one faculty member observed the essential role of a common authentic task: "You don't know that you're speaking a different language when you're just speaking. You have to do something in order to find it out." The same faculty member went on to suggest that only through engaging in common, real tasks will the language needs appear:

We would talk about definitions of inquiry and definitions of information technology and everybody thought they were on the same page. But [when] we actually were trying to articulate what was happening in the science labs . . . and what was happening in education, and trying to work together . . . to accomplish a goal, that was when we found out we didn't understand.

Common Purpose. The importance of authentic tasks to effective learning environments is well recognized (Bransford, Brown, & Cocking, 2000). In the classroom, we know that students more readily engage in learning when the problems they are solving are relevant to their lives, not just abstract learning goals. Teachers will more willingly participate in professional development experiences that provide them with materials or strategies that address their real classroom challenges (Putnam & Borko, 2000). It stands to reason that the same would hold true for those collaborating on the design and implementation of professional development.

Within the ITS Learning Ecology, the yearly synergistic inquiry experience took on the function of common purpose or task. Over time that purpose evolved from providing practitioners with an authentic science experience to providing such an experience *and* supporting them in transporting some aspect of that experience to their classroom (see Chapter 4). That evolution in focus required a shift in the way that the science and education faculty interacted with one another, prompting them away from mere coordination into cooperation and toward collaboration. At first, the division of responsibilities was such that the work of scientists and educators remained separate—like parallel play with a common goal. However, as practitioners came to insist on greater integration of their learning experiences and greater relevance to their classrooms for the products they were producing, faculty found themselves readily crossing the cultural divide in an effort to support the practitioners' learning. The evolving design and implementation of the synergistic research experience from year to year was a good indicator of the ITS Learning Ecology's growth over 6 years from a group of individuals and individual teams to a collaborative working and learning environment.

Room for Play; Room for Change. An important component in establishing a *culture apart* is opportunity for experimentation. The scientists and education specialists were free to develop their respective portions of the synergistic inquiry experience for practitioners within very flexible guidelines. Scientists who said that they had been "thinking about doing things" in their undergraduate classes were encouraged and supported in their efforts to explore more effective ways of conveying their knowledge to grade 7–16 practitioners. This freedom and respect for individual paths to a common goal seemed to promote a sense of ownership in the program and a willingness to take on a very substantial role in both planning and implementation of the inquiry experience. As one faculty member put it:

One of the strengths of the project was that there was such an emphasis on openness. . . . There wasn't one preset idea of "this is what we're going to do, we're going to accomplish it, it's a contract and we're just gonna implement the model as is." There was a lot of opportunity for growth.

Supporting such an environment requires leadership that is responsive yet not directive. The director's relaxed style of management and willingness to let others participate in meaningful ways in the design and direction of the synergistic inquiry experience seemed to foster a distributed sense of responsibility and ownership in the project. A science faculty member explained:

The leadership makes a big difference. [The director] was very good at knowing when to pressure people to attend things and when to back off and let them exercise their own judgment. . . . [The director] also made sure that everyone was getting listened to, which facilitates that climate of respect.

By Year 3, there was evidence of substantial buy-in among faculty who worked well beyond their required time commitment to the project and attended committee meetings out of interest rather than obligation. One scientist declared himself "willing to do this even without pay." And while this was never put to the test, it is worth noting that unlike some projects that are "director-driven" and dependent on the zeal and energy of one or two individuals, in this project the expertise and leadership came to rest on distributed drive and a sense of community.

Of course, distributed leadership and room to explore bring us back to the need for the *right people*. To cultivate such an environment, one faculty member gave the following insight: "I think you have to have people who think this is fun. Part of the fun of it is that you are creating it as you go. There isn't a formula. And . . . that's frustrating for a lot of people. [Y]ou have to have people who don't mind that."

PRINCIPLES OF COMPLEXITY APPLIED TO AN IT-BASED LEARNING ECOLOGY

In the previous section, some of the principles of organizational theory allowed us to explain the particular *hows* and *whys* of the successful development of an innovative university partnership. However, as Fullan (1999) has pointed out, "Even when you know what research and published advice has to say you will not know exactly how to apply it to your particular situation with its unique problems and opportunities" (p. 29). This has been confirmed in research and in our own experience in evaluation. When asked to identify the lessons learned, project staff and leadership are often skeptical that what they have lived can be reverse-engineered. They talk about how the project grew organically and how what they learned occurred through a process they could not have predicted in advance.

The typical lessons learned from large projects rarely present future groups with a blueprint for success. No number of linear logic models will help them to avoid the pitfalls inherent in bringing diverse groups of people together to work toward a common goal. The principles of organizational theory, so prevalent in partnership literature, are not sufficient for describing dynamic, transitory communities such as these short-term partnerships. Success, failure, movement, and stasis are all factors inherent in the creation and adoption of innovation (Lemke & Sabelli, 2008). However, the current approaches to evaluation and design of these projects do not easily record this development. More recent theory provides additional insights into development of complex learning communities (e.g., Davis & Simmt, 2003).

There has been some attempt to apply systems theory research to evaluation of large-scale educational reform projects. Contagion dynamics, for example, has been applied to the dissemination of innovations within educational programs (Young, 2007). But as Lemke and colleagues have recently pointed out, there are challenges to accurately modeling educational systems before we can hope to leverage the research on complex systems to look at change within those systems.

There may, however, be an interim strategy. In the last few years, researchers in mathematics education have applied complexity science to looking at the complex learning systems of formal and informal learning environments. Davis and Simmt (2003) draw on the principles of *internal diversity, redundancy, decentralized control, organized randomness,* and *neighbor interactions work* to re-describe a small online mathematical learning community and to prescribe conditions (as opposed to strategies) to promote an ITS Learning Ecology within a mathematics classroom. Those same principles, as we hope to illustrate, may also provide a promising framework for looking at even larger learning ecologies, such as a school–university partnership.

There is no room here to adequately describe the history of complexity science or even elaborate appropriately on each of the principles listed above that we discuss in this section. However, we hope to illustrate their promise in re-laying the nature of complex productive social learning environments such as educational partnerships. In the process, we draw heavily on the work of Davis and Simmt (2003) and their application of these concepts to mathematics-related learning environments—especially as they employ complexity principles to describe the development of a learning community of mathematics teachers.

Complexity science was born out of several areas of research in the physical sciences (e.g., systems theory, cybernetics, artificial intelligence) and has grown to include the study of any living system from the human body to social systems.

Complex systems all share the attributes of adaptability, self-organization, and emergence; they are essentially *learning systems* (Capra, 1996; Johnson, 2001), where learning is understood as a recursive process of adaptation through which systems develop and maintain their coherences (Davis & Simmt, 2003).

Complex systems may be best understood by comparing them to simple systems, which involve only a few interacting objects. Simple systems can be explained in mechanical terms of inputs and outputs, and they are relatively predictable. Complex systems, on the other hand, are large, involve multiple agents, and are both self-organizing and adaptable to new situations. Complex systems are commonly referred to as learning systems because they can grow and adapt to circumstances as those circumstances change. And while they may not be entirely unpredictable, these systems are not easily described in mechanistic terms. In light of these definitions, it seems increasingly illogical to employ linear *logic models* to describe the design and development of nonlinear complex systems.

In the next section, we look at the potential utility of applying the principles of complexity science to describe learning systems consisting of university faculty, graduate students, grade 7–12 practitioners, and administrators (or any combination) that evolve (or not) into creative communities that achieve the goals of a project. For each component, we provide a brief explanation of its meaning, a brief discussion of Davis and Simmt's (2003) application to learning environments, and examples of how it might be extended to examine educational partnerships.

Internal Diversity

The intelligence and creativity of a system—and consequently its ability to learn and adapt to new situations—are largely linked to its internal diversity. We readily understand this notion in the context of nature, where we have recently been faced with several crises of imbalance due to a lack of diversity. We are seeing, for example, the negative effects of industrial monoculture farming and the rampant takeover of certain species when natural predators have been eliminated through disease or hunting. We are used to the importance of distributed expertise in the fields of business and education. However, the notion of internal diversity coupled with redundancy is potentially a more fruitful way of regarding essential components of a program because we can apply the concepts not only to the people involved but also to the processes and procedures that support the community and its production.

Davis and Simmt (2003) emphasize that "one cannot specify in advance what sorts of variation will be necessary for appropriately intelligent action, hence the need to ensure the presence of diversity" (p. 148). This is important in terms of who turned out to be the right people for the project. As noted earlier, in selecting the scientists who would participate in the design and implementation of the synergistic inquiry experiences, the choice of intelligent novices over experts in teacher education for the SLCs appeared to be the best option for attaining a creative incorporation of authentic science into an integrated inquiry experience. On the other hand, diversity at the programmatic level—a combination of science and education experts—proved to be a good formula for stretching creative thinking for the translation of authentic science experiences to grade 7–16 science classrooms.

Davis and Simmt (2003) also caution that one cannot impose diversity in the form of organized formal classroom roles (e.g., facilitator, note taker); rather, diversity must be assumed and flexible. We witnessed this at both the ITS Learning Ecology level and the SLC level. Early in the project, some of the SLCs attempted to assign an education role to one individual who would presumably help the practitioners translate their learning to classroom-based projects. We watched as that role was eventually taken on by other individuals within the project. Practitioners did not naturally or regularly go to the person charged with the role of education translator on the team. Instead, they gravitated toward education faculty members or particular graduate students and other practitioners they felt could appropriately support their efforts. The flexibility of the project's leadership allowed for this; over the years, what had begun as a specific SLC role became the role of various members of the community.

Redundancy

Redundancy refers to the "duplication and excesses of the sorts of features that are necessary to particular events" (Davis & Simmt, 2003, p. 150). This concept is related to stability and coherence in a learning system in two key ways. First, it facilitates interactions among agents in the system; second, it allows for agents to compensate for one another's shortcomings.

In their online community of teacher learners, Davis and Simmt (2003) similarly found that *sameness* among participants (e.g., similar culturally, professionally, educationally) was essential in "triggering a transition from a collection of 'mes' to a collective of us" (p. 150). We have similar findings from this project. As mentioned earlier, the faculty involved came from a single institution, which provided a more or less common infrastructure, rewards system, resources, and academic schedule—something that has posed considerable challenges to inter-institutional and virtual partnerships. One could even say that the larger participating cultures of science and education were replicated within the community of graduate students. This contributed substantially to developing a common vision and language for communicating the work of the ITS Learning Ecology as well as fostering communication among the faculty cultures.

In our experience evaluating educational projects, we have found that redundancy in background in a collaborative effort can support the development of or sustain a common vision. (Common vision may even be regarded as an example of redundancy.) At the risk of stretching the interpretation of this concept, we also observed that redundancy of efforts and focus is also critical to attaining program and project goals.

Elsewhere we argued that goal strands within a project (e.g., attention to learner diversity, practitioner diversity, technology for learning, and formative assessment) require a designated champion if they are to succeed. However, the success or failure of that goal then becomes largely dependent on the expertise of the champion and the extent to which she or he is empowered within the system. For instance, another project we worked with had as one of its goals the increase of ethnic diversity in the pool of science teachers in the region. Over 6 years, that goal had several false starts and ultimately was never realized. In the ITS Learning Ecology, the champion of information technology in education left early on (although for a while provided counsel from a distance). The technology goal became less specific and less prominent for a time. Responsibility for the success of that particular goal had been largely dependent on the expertise and efforts of a single individual. In the first case (that of achieving ethnic diversity), the absence of a champion resulted in failure; in the second case (the ITS Learning Ecology), the reliance on a single individual to lead the effort turned out to be fragile. Thinking in terms of redundancy would prompt us to seek out multiple individuals and resources committed to a project strand to ensure its steady growth within the project.

Thinking in terms of redundancy rather than individual champions also forces us to think beyond just people to the many processes and procedures (in place or to be developed) necessary to bring a particular project goal to fruition. Looking at the design of a project and its allotment of resources (appropriately redundant?) could therefore provide some indication of potential success or failure at all points in its development.

Neighbor Interactions

Within a mathematics class community, Davis and Simmt (2003) found that:

> "Neighbors" were not physical bodies or social groupings . . . rather . . . these neighbors that must "bump" up against one another are ideas, hunches, queries, and other manners of representation. . . . The researchers also found that there must be "sufficient density" of such interactions to result in the community learning/evolving. (p. 156)

This makes sense on an intuitive level, where we might think in terms of needing a tipping point of interaction to prompt the adoption of a new practice or way of thinking.

The concept of neighbor interactions also has obvious implications for project design, as the opportunities and mechanisms for these to occur must be consciously included. Within the ITS Learning Ecology, science and education graduate students catalyzed many of the neighbor interactions. The influence of these year-round members of the ITS Learning Ecology cannot be underestimated. Some of their interactions, shared ideas, and research predated that of the corresponding education and science faculty. The evolving role of the graduate students within the ITS Learning Ecology helped to catalyze the communications between the education and science portions of the project. Beginning as practitioners or graduate student participants in the summer program, they later became co-facilitators of the entire inquiry experience. Consequently, graduate students both *lived* and *languaged* the integration of these two sides of the project into a coherent whole.

Decentralized Control and Organized Randomness

Decentralized control and organized randomness provide the underlying ground rules for the ITS Learning Ecology. The two work together to provide room for neighbor interactions to take place, which is perhaps why we feel compelled to combine them for discussion here. Within the emergent community of mathematics teachers, Davis and Simmt (2003) observed that "there was no overseer, no director. The collective emerged and sustained itself through shared projects, not through planning or other deliberate management strategies" (p. 152). Decision making and direction setting were shared or distributed across members. In other words, there was decentralized control. Nevertheless, the authors are quick to point out that this does not imply that anything goes. Rather, they observe the need for complex systems to maintain a delicate balance between organization and randomness.

Decentralized control and organized randomness seem to correspond to what we described in the first half of this chapter as room for play and decentralized leadership. In both cases, we are describing circumstances that prompt discussion, exploration and experimentation (i.e., neighbor interactions), and transformation. However, the notion of decentralized control seems more powerful as it at once suggests both enactment and direction. Moreover, it can be applied to all levels of decision making and organization within a collaborative project—not just the directorship. Similarly, the notion of organized randomness might be expanded to include project goals or principles and other ground rules for group operation.

SUMMARY

Successful educational partnerships are often described in retrospect as evolving from a combination of careful design and serendipity. Can partnership success be reverse-engineered? Drawing on lessons learned from multiple university–school partnerships, the literature from organizational theory, and principles extracted from complex systems theory, this chapter described components critical to creating an integrated program that promotes the development of a productive, interdependent learning environment.

Diversity of the membership of interdisciplinary groups calls for the creation of structures, knowledge, tools, and processes that both accommodate and mediate the various professional cultures of origin. We described how having the right people who share a common place and history as they work toward creating a functional culture apart from their original cultures resulted in an effective learning community. From complexity theory we extracted principles to provide additional insights into the development of complex learning environments. Internal diversity, redundancy of efforts and expertise, opportunities for neighbor interactions, and decentralized control with organized randomness all combined to create the conditions needed for successful development of the ITS Learning Ecology.

REFERENCES

Bransford, J., Brown, A., & Cocking, R. (Eds.). (2000). *How people learn: Brain, mind, experience, and school* (expanded ed.). Washington, DC: National Academy Press.

Bruer, J. T. (1993). *Schools for thought: A science of learning in the classroom.* Cambridge, MA: MIT Press.

Capra, F. (1996). *The web of life: A new scientific understanding of living things.* New York: Doubleday.

Davis, B., & Simmt, E. (2003). Understanding learning systems: Mathematics education and complexity science. *Journal for Research in Mathematics Education, 34*(2), 137–167.

Fullan, M. (1999). *Change forces: The sequel.* New York: Routledge.

Johnson, S. (2001). *Emergence: The connected lives of ants, brains, cities and software.* New York: Scribner.

Kingsley, G., & Waschak, M. R. (2005, September). *Finding value and meaning in the concept partnership.* Paper presented at the MSP Evaluation Summit: Evidence-Based Findings from MSP's, Minneapolis, MN.

Lemke, J. L., & Sabelli, N. H. (2008). Complex systems and educational change: Towards a new research agenda. *Educational Philosophy and Theory, 40*(1), 118–129.

Looi, C. K. (2001). Enhancing learning ecologies on the Internet. *Journal of Computer Assisted Learning, 17,* 13–20.

Putnam, R., & Borko, H. (2000). What do new views of knowledge and thinking have to say about research on teacher learning? *Educational Researcher, 29*(1), 4–15.

Sirotnik, K., & Goodlad, J. (1988). *School–university partnerships in action: Concepts, cases, and concerns.* New York: Teachers College Press.

Slater, J. (2001). The process of change in school–university collaboration. In R. Ravid & M. G. Handler (Eds.), *The many faces of school–university collaboration: Characteristics of successful partnerships* (pp. 11–22). Portsmouth, NH: Teacher Ideas Press.

Wittengenstein, L. (1918). *Tractatus logico-philosophicus.* Retrieved September 26, 2010, from http://www.gutenberg.org/files/5740/5740-h/5740-h.htm

Young, H. P. (2007). *Innovative differences in heterogeneous populations.* New York: Brookings Center on Social and Economic Dynamics.

About the Editors
and the Contributors

Jane F. Schielack is a Professor in the Mathematics Department and Associate Dean for Assessment and Pre-K–12 Education in the College of Science at Texas A&M University. A member of the Texas A&M faculty since 1982, Schielack received both her BS and PhD degrees (1975, 1988) in mathematics education from Texas A&M University. She earned an MA in mathematics education from the University of Texas in 1980. In 2006, she led a National Council of Teachers of Mathematics writing team that developed focal points designed to guide curricula to better prepare U.S. elementary and middle school students for high school and eventual careers in science and engineering. She served as the Director of the NSF-funded Information Technology in Science (ITS) Center for Teaching and Learning. Her research interests include mathematics curriculum development and the uses of multiple representations, including those created with technology, to learn mathematics in grades K–8.

Stephanie L. Knight is a Professor in the Department of Educational Psychology, Counseling, and Special Education at Pennsylvania State University. She received her BA in Romance Languages and Literature from the University of Kentucky, her MA in Secondary Education from Lehigh University, and her doctorate in Curriculum and Instruction from the University of Houston. Prior to joining the faculty at Penn State, she was at Texas A&M University, where she held the Houston Endowment, Inc., Endowed Chair in Urban Education and received a university award for outstanding teaching. She is currently editor of the *Journal of Teacher Education* and was previously co-editor of the Teaching, Learning, and Human Development section of the *American Educational Research Journal*. Her research interests include the impact of classroom processes on student outcomes and pre-service and in-service teacher professional development. She has published numerous books, chapters, and journal articles in these areas and was named a University Faculty Fellow at Texas A&M in recognition of her scholarship. Dr. Knight teaches graduate and undergraduate courses in educational psychology and teacher education at Penn State.

Gillian Acheson. Associate Professor of Geography, Southern Illinois University at Edwardsville, Edwardsville, Illinois. Former ITS Center Graduate Research Assistant.

Ruth Anderson. Educational Researcher, FACET Innovations, LLC., Seattle, Washington. Former ITS Center External Evaluator.

Lawrence Griffing. Associate Professor of Biology, Texas A&M University. Former ITS Associate Director for Life Sciences and Project Team Leader for two teams: (1) Macro (Grizzly Bear) and Micro (Plant Cell) Imaging and (2) Plant Genomics and Time-Lapse Imaging.

Bruce Herbert. Professor of Geology and Geophysics, Texas A&M University. Former ITS Center Associate Director for Geosciences and Science Project Team Leader for the Sustained Coastal Margins Team.

Margaret Hobson. Assistant Director for Outreach, Office of Strategic Research Development, Texas Engineering Experiment Station. Former ITS Center Participant.

Cathleen C. Loving. Associate Professor of Teaching, Learning, and Culture, Texas A&M University. Former ITS Center Associate Director for Research in Science Literacy.

Karen McNeal. Assistant Professor of Geology, Mississippi State University. Former ITS Center Graduate Research Assistant.

Jim Minstrell. Research Scientist, FACET Innovations, LLC, Seattle, Washington. Former ITS Center External Evaluator.

George M. Nickles. Assistant to the Dean for Technology and Curriculum, College of Education and Allied Professions, Western Carolina University. Former ITS Center Director of Evaluation.

Susan Pedersen. Associate Professor of Educational Psychology, Texas A&M University. Former ITS Center Associate Director for Educational Technologies.

Carol Stuessy. Associate Professor of Teaching, Learning, and Culture. Former ITS Center Associate Director for Research in Science Learning Environments.

X. Ben Wu. Professor of Ecosystem Science and Management, Associate Dean of Faculties, and Director of the Center for Teaching Excellence, Texas A&M University. Former ITS Center Science Project Team Leader for the Landscape Ecology Team.

Index

Note: Page numbers followed by **f** and **t** represent figures and tables respectively.